Keep Your Eye on the

Marshmallow!

Berkley titles by Joachim de Posada

AND ELLEN SINGER

Don't Eat the Marshmallow . . . Yet!
Don't Gobble the Marshmallow . . . Ever!

AND BOB ANDELMAN

Keep Your Eye on the Marshmallow!

Keep Your Eye on the
Marshmallow!

Gain Focus and Resilience—
And Come Out Ahead

Joachim de Posada
and Bob Andelman

B

BERKLEY BOOKS, NEW YORK

THE BERKLEY PUBLISHING GROUP
Published by the Penguin Group
Penguin Group (USA) Inc.
375 Hudson Street, New York, New York 10014, USA

USA I Canada I UK I Ireland I Australia I New Zealand I India I South Africa I China

Penguin Books Ltd., Registered Offices: 80 Strand, London WC2R 0RL, England
For more information about the Penguin Group, visit penguin.com.

This book is an original publication of The Berkley Publishing Group.

Library of Congress Cataloging-in-Publication Data

Posada, Joachim de.
Keep your eye on the marshmallow! : gain focus and resilience—and come out ahead
/ Joachim de Posada and Bob Andelman. — First edition.
p. cm
ISBN 978-0-425-24739-6
1. Success.   2. Goal (Psychology)   3. Success in business.   I. Andelman, Bob.
II. Title.
BF637.S8P59847 2013
650.1—dc23
2012048452

FIRST EDITION: May 2013

PRINTED IN THE UNITED STATES OF AMERICA

10   9   8   7   6   5   4   3   2   1

The publisher does not have any control over and does not assume any responsibility for author or third-party websites or their content.

ALWAYS LEARNING   PEARSON

This book is dedicated to my daughter, Caroline; her husband, Orlando; my three grandkids, Orly, Justin, and Ryan; my mother, Carmita; and to Aisha, my life partner.

Acknowledgments

Joachim de Posada

A big thank-you to all members of our team: Bob Andelman for doing a fantastic job as my coauthor; literary
agents Jane Dystel, Miriam Goderich, and Lauren
Abramo for their fine work representing my interests; and
editor Denise Silvestro for having faith in our third
Marshmallow book and graciously extending the deadline
because of unforeseen circumstances.

Thanks, also, to my daughter, Caroline, who is my
rock, for being there for me always, without exception.
She motivates me in every area of my life and has given
me two beautiful grandsons, Orlando Joaquin and Justin
Gonzalo, who inspire me every day of my life.

To my mother, who I love with all my heart and who
still treats me as a kid.

My sister, Patty, and her husband, Manuel, who allow me to stay in their beautiful home in Westport, Connecticut, anytime I need to meet with my agents or publishers and whenever I have a speech in New York City. Thank you!

To Aisha, the woman in my life, who I love dearly and is with me all the time, supporting me 100 percent in all that I do—even when I write until four or five in the morning.

Writers and speakers constantly need new ideas and I would like to thank the members of the two mastermind groups with whom I regularly meet: Bruce Turkel, Rebecca Staton-Reinstein, Helen Turnbull, Mace Horoff, Ken Akers, Rick Goodman, Robert Stack, and Alicia Bain. My other and most recent mastermind group: Terry Brock, Randy Gage, Lisa Jimenez, Bob Burg, Gina Carr, Kathy Zader, and Patrick K. Stinus.

Thank you to my partners: Ramon Arias, president of InterAmerican Consultants, with whom I have been associated for seventeen years; Jorge Fernandez, who works with me directly in my company, Dr. Joachim de Posada and Associates, Inc.; and Frances Rios, my strategic partner in Puerto Rico and my mentee in the speaking business.

And to all my dear friends and followers online who constantly write me with ideas, constructive criticism, and much-needed comments about my books or speeches.

Finally, my everlasting appreciation to every human being who inhabits this world with the intention of leaving Planet Earth in better shape than they found it and who always tries to construct instead of destroy.

Bob Andelman

My career as a coauthor relies on finding good, smart people with interesting stories to tell. Joachim de Posada is definitely one of those folks. We found an easy rapport from day one. I greatly enjoyed the process of writing this book alongside him, profiting from his insights and good humor.

I would never have met Joachim if not for a recommendation from my agent, Jane Dystel of Dystel & Goderich Literary Management, and I continue to be in her debt for successfully playing matchmaker. (I also appreciate ongoing support at the agency from Miriam Goderich, Lauren Abramo, and Michael Bourret.)

It has been a pleasure working with and getting to know our delightful editor, Denise Silvestro.

Jana Ward joined me as a transcriber with this project

and what a great addition to the team she is: hardworking, attentive to details, and conscientious about deadlines. Thank you, Jana—and our mutual friend Kim Caswell, who introduced us.

Joachim and I live five hours apart by car, so we needed a middle ground to meet. That became the Hilton Garden Inn near the Fort Myers, Florida, airport. We asked the staff for permission to meet in a corner of the lobby and they graciously allowed us to hash out much of the spine of this book there. Thanks! And just across the street from the Hilton, at the Gulf Coast Town Center, we became fans of the made-to-order charburgers (and milkshakes for Joachim!) at Foster's Grille. *Yum.*

Finally, I always acknowledge the support of my wife, Mimi, and my daughter, Rachel, as writing each book creates its own stresses on a household. But I couldn't do what I do without the long-distance enthusiasm of my mother, Phyllis, my sister, Lori Parsells, and my brother, Ira. Thank you all.

Contents

Contents

Joachim's Pre-Parable Analysis

Have you ever noticed that some days, the greatest challenge in life starts with making your goals and desires square with those of someone else?

Maybe it's a spouse or a partner; maybe it's a boss or the person in the cubicle next to you. It could just as easily be the straphanger next to you on the morning train or the driver alongside you rushing to get home tonight.

Some days we all struggle to make the right choices, the ones that will allow us to pursue our own life, liberty, and happiness without detracting from the desires of someone right next to us.

When we last saw the hero of the first two *Marshmallow* guides to success, *Don't Eat the Marshmallow . . . Yet!* and *Don't Gobble the Marshmallow . . . Ever!*, Arthur had emerged from extreme personal and financial situations that challenged his adherence to our basic tenet: Don't eat your marshmallow . . . yet!

Life was good again for Arthur at the end of book two. He married the love of his life, Akilah. They had twins on the way. Career opportunities for Arthur—after a rough start—were strong, and former waitress Akilah became her own boss after opening a restaurant she called Just Ask.

If only life reached a pleasant plateau and stayed there, right?

But we all know it doesn't work that way. I often remember the late comedienne Gilda Radner's words: "I wanted a perfect ending. Now I've learned, the hard way, that some poems don't rhyme, and some stories don't have a clear beginning, middle, and end. Life is about not knowing, having to change, taking the moment and making the best of it, without knowing what's going to happen next."

Eight years have passed in Arthur's world and he thinks it's time for a change. But the global economy is coming out of its worst malaise since the Great Depression of the 1930s. Arthur has ambition; he has heart. But he might still have some old bad habits to overcome, which is why his wife isn't so sure it's the right time to strike out on his own. Maybe one entrepreneur—*her*—is enough for their family?

• • •

Millions of people around the world have already read at least one of the first two Marshmallow books. I have received e-mail from many of you and talked to thousands more every year at speaking engagements and book signings. And one of the questions I hear most often repeated is this:

> *I believed in the marshmallow theory when I was single, but making it work in a marriage (or business partnership) is much tougher. How can I stick with its principles when so many of life's decisions must be made with—and in consideration of—another person?*

It's a great question, one I have often faced in my own life.

And, ironically, it's one we discover that Arthur is now facing in his own life! (Quite a coincidence, right?)

Following marshmallow principles was not always easy for Arthur when he was a single man with no responsibilities to anyone other than himself. But now he must make choices in support of his position as the head of a household. Every choice he makes, every marshmallow he savors or gobbles affects his wife, their two children, and even the family dog.

His two career mentors, Jonathan Patient and Charlie Slow, are still in the picture, providing strong support, but they may believe it's time for Arthur to stand on his own two feet. Does he?

As we return to observe Arthur's life today, we see a seemingly successful executive, loving husband, and father.

And yet . . .

For those who haven't read my first two *Marshmallow* books, I encourage you to get them so that you can follow the story from the beginning. That said, we are writing this book so that it stands alone. In other words, you don't need to have read the others to grasp the wonderful and effective principles we will discuss in this one.

Let's review the basis for marshmallow logic and the principle behind it.

Years ago, an American psychologist named Walter Mischel conducted a simple, yet fascinating experiment with 643 four-year-old children. Mischel and his colleagues sat them down in a room, one by one, and placed a marshmallow on a table in front of them. Mischel told each child that he needed to leave the room for fifteen minutes and when he came back, if the marshmallow was there on the table, he would give the child another one. If the child ate the marshmallow, experiment over—no more marshmallows! If the child didn't eat it, he or she received a second one. That was a 100 percent return on investment in fifteen minutes, not bad at all, even for a four-year-old. The problem? Telling a four-year-old child to wait fifteen minutes to get something he or she wanted *now*. That was equivalent to telling an adult to wait three hours for a cup of coffee. It is rather a long time.

So what happened?

Two out of three children ate the marshmallow. Some did it after five seconds, a minute, two minutes, others lasted longer, holding out up to thirteen minutes.

But one out of three kids *didn't* eat the marshmallow. He or she would look at it, put it back, even lick it, but not eat it. Already at age four, that child understood the most important principle of success: self-discipline—the ability to delay gratification.

Fourteen years later, there was a follow-up study. Researchers were able to locate many of the kids who participated in the original study, now eighteen- and nineteen-year-old young men and women.

What did they discover about them?

The kids who hadn't eaten the marshmallows at four were doing well. They were in college, their entrance exam grades—the SAT and ACT—were, on average, 213 points higher than those of the kids who ate the marshmallows. They enjoyed good relationships with teachers, fellow students, and their parents. They were well-adjusted kids who exhibited greater levels of self-control than their marshmallow-gobbling counterparts.

Many of the kids who ate the marshmallows, however, hadn't made it to college and were working at low-level jobs, making little money and spending a lot more than they earned. Some made it to college and dropped out; some were in college with poor grades, and only a few were succeeding.

Along with intelligence, and a little bit of luck, the marshmallow principle of self-control and the ability to delay gratification proved a strong predictor of success. (We will discuss another important predictor, the Grit Factor, later on.)

Have you ever bought a book, audiobook, or DVD or attended a seminar that promised to teach you a vital new skill, make you rich, help you lose every pound you need to lose, and turn you into a champion of relationship building?

Armed with this fresh knowledge, your business and personal hopes were raised. Reenergized, you drew up new career and life plans.

But . . . if change failed to materialize quickly, you lost faith and gave up on your radical new plans and expectations. Life returned to normal. Normal, in some cases, consisted of shallow breathing and tightly wound nerves, working a dead-end job from nine to five that sometimes kept you from becoming homeless but little more.

In this book, we want to tell you how to use self-discipline and different thinking to change yourself for the better. We will present you with ideas to focus you on what you want and to aid you in becoming resilient enough that you can succeed in any hard times that might be around the corner. As a benefit, self-discipline and the ability to change your thinking patterns will let you relax because you will be able to remove a big percentage of stress, leaving your mind ready to handle the important challenges in all areas of your life in good times or bad.

But I must be honest with you: Acquiring self-control, focus, and resiliency, or thinking in original or creative ways is not as simple as some self-help books purport it to be. You can't just wish your way to success. You need to take some action: Be aware of your weaknesses, remain vigilant against falling back into bad habits, and move toward your goals with steadfast focus, always keeping in mind your long-term desires.

However, even people with incredible focus fall into a common trap that causes success and happiness to elude them. Their big mistake is they concentrate on one area of life at the expense of everything else. They spend all their waking hours concentrating on career and forget little things such as calling a parent, paying attention to their children or ever reading a book for the sheer pleasure of it.

While career advancement and financial health are important, there is much more to life. Success, then, is not just a measure of how financially independent you are; it's about having strong, mutually beneficial relationships; passion for your job, career or hobby; good health; and a vision that goes further than your own life or family, into your community, country or even the world. We call this state of success "well-being."

In *Keep Your Eye on the Marshmallow!*, we give you tools, knowledge, and know-how that will advance your life and help you achieve that elusive state called well-being. We will teach you how to, in effect, rewire your brain so that you start processing events in a different manner.

Just remember, the biggest single obstacle to your own well-being is *YOU*. We all allow our need for immediate gratification to override what is best for us.

Incidentally, I think this need for instant gratification is part of our culture. We want what we want, and we want it now. I believe this is a major reason why the United States, once a leader in education, technology, scientific advancement, etc., is now falling behind. Compare us to our counterparts in many Asian countries: Self-discipline and focus account for much of the success they achieve. The people in these countries embrace the marshmallow message and live by its principles. Maybe this is why the *Marshmallow* books have done so well there. *Don't Eat the Marshmallow . . . Yet!* became a number one bestseller in Korea and remained in that position for more than sixty weeks. The sequel, *Don't Gobble the Marshmallow . . . Ever!*, also made it to number one. Both books also sold several million copies in Taiwan, China, and other countries around the globe.

Think about how we Americans live our lives. Too many of us eat too much, work too much, and exercise too little.

We all purport to know that doing a fair amount of exercise three or four times a week will have a very positive impact on our health, right? Yet we stop exercising soon after we start, preferring to sit in front of a television set collecting dust and cobwebs watching the latest episodes of *CSI*.

Sooner or later, we will have a stroke or a heart attack that could have been prevented. Talk about a crime! Skipping one day won't kill us but sooner or later we will get hit.

We know it is important to eat the right foods, yet we consume too much processed sugar, eat too many fried foods, and drink too much alcohol. In this (sugar and fried foods, not alcohol, thank goodness), I am as guilty as the next person; every meal is a struggle, a new set of right or wrong decisions to be made.

And how many of us work too much, spending way too much time at the office and away from the people who are most important to us? And with technology, even when we're home we're constantly working. We're connected to e-mail 24/7, always on, always working, always trying to get ahead.

As a professional speaker and workaholic, I have traveled all my life and I know that this has sometimes negatively affected my family. I, however, made sure that my daughter understood what I did for a living and how I made a difference in millions of people's lives.

One day, when she was just a child, I made her three promises. I said, "Caroline, you know that I do what I do because it is my passion, because I help so many people around the world. But I want to promise you three things: (1) I will call you every day no matter what country I am in; (2) I will also send you a postcard from every city or country in which I speak; and (3) You and I will attend the convention of the National Speakers Association every year, together. You will go to the youth program and I will attend the adult one and at night we will compare notes. It will be our annual, high quality, learning mini-vacation." We did it for twelve years in a row.

Imagine my surprise when my daughter, now a grown woman with two beautiful little boys, one day presented me with a huge surprise.

Out came a big box in which she'd saved every single postcard, letter, and personal note I'd written to her since she was a little girl. Tears rolled down my face at the time; in fact, writing about it now, my eyes are getting misty all over again. She said that, thanks to those phone calls and postcards, she always felt I was with her even if we were thousands of miles apart. We went through some of the postcards, in which I gave her advice, told her about some of my experiences, or simply described something beautiful about the country I was visiting.

We were so caught up in that moment that we didn't notice my son-in-law watching us intently while he sat on the couch next to us. He suddenly said, "Now I understand."

We looked at him and almost in unison said, "Now you understand *what?*"

He went on to say that he understood why Caroline and I had such a special and profound father-daughter relationship when few of my daughter's girlfriends, some of whose parents were still married, did. He then gave us a wonderful idea and a definite challenge: "You must write a book about it. You have to teach millions of parents who are divorced how to raise their kids with love and with an important presence in their children's lives." So, my dear readers, soon you will be able to read the book we are writing: *Love, Dad.*

When you plant a seed, watering and fertilizing it daily, a beautiful flower comes out of the ground. My daughter, the person I most admire in my life, is now a prominent attorney, a marvelous young woman and an out-of-this-world mother. That, my friends, is my greatest success.

Now, without further ado, let's check in with Arthur and learn how keeping our eye on the marshmallow can enable us all to succeed.

1

Husband, Father . . . Marshmallow Man?

Orly's eyes grew wide as saucers when Arthur got home from work every night.

It was always a race for the door between him and the family's English bulldog, Chief, to see who would be there first to greet the man of the house.

No matter what kind of day he had just completed at the office or on the road, selling products for SlowDown! Inc. and sharing his marshmallow logic with the world of business, nonprofits and world governments, Arthur knew there would always be at least one person—and one tail-wagging canine—who couldn't wait to see him cross the threshold at home.

The eight-year-old boy and his faithful companion always leapt from wherever they were perched in the family's Coral Gables town house when they heard Arthur's key in the front door.

Arthur's pulse quickened every time he heard the squeal, "Daddy's home!" followed by barking, footsteps, and paws on the tile in the foyer. Orly always opened the door before Arthur's key could finish the job. Arthur then scooped his son up with one arm, dropping his briefcase and petting the equally excited dog with his other hand.

"Oh, Daddy, wait until I tell you what Justin did today!" he'd say, bursting to share the details of his twin brother's latest adventures and the indignities Justin perpetrated upon him.

While Orly and Chief opened the show, Akilah and Justin were the second act, meeting them halfway to the living room where Justin would try to act cool and nod to his father, knowing that his twin would soon spill the beans on his latest infraction.

As for Akilah, she would always give her husband of ten years a peck on the cheek. Arthur noticed that some days the peck was less enthusiastic than others. As a couple—like any other—they definitely had their good days and bad;

if she leaned into him and put a hand on the small of his back while doing so, he knew it was a good day; otherwise, he knew it might be a long, unpleasant night.

When he sensed one of those nights coming on, he frequented the kitchen more often, snacking on salty treats or dinner leftovers, chugging sugary soft drinks, or finishing off whatever rich desserts might be calling to him from the refrigerator.

He found food a way of mentally drifting off without physically leaving the room whenever Akilah began one of her lectures about how he wasn't paying enough attention to her and the kids, or wondering when he was going to be his own man instead of slaving away as someone else's employee.

Arthur *was* his own man—in his own mind, at least; he was the Marshmallow Man. And that was enough for him—for at least a little while longer.

Arthur was doing very well at SlowDown! Inc. He was consistently one of their top salespeople, and he knew his boss, Mr. Slow, was quite fond of him. And the job had become a no-brainer. Arthur could practically do it in his sleep. What more could he ask for?

The truth was, Arthur did want more. He thought every day about being his own boss. In fact, he thought so much about it, sometimes it seemed that's all he ever thought about. He had so many questions: Could he do it? Could he really succeed at being self-employed? What if he failed? What would he do then? Would Akilah leave him? Would Mr. Slow take him back? So many doubts—they bounced around in his head, making him dizzy. Arthur was unable to do anything but think some more.

2

Squeezing the Marshmallow

Charlie Slow, president and founder of SlowDown! Inc., had always liked Arthur. From the start, he saw something special in the young man and wanted to see it develop and bloom.

But that was several years ago already. Mr. Slow had always expected Arthur to be someone who would learn all he could at SlowDown! Inc., then go out into the world and do something even greater with his talents and abilities.

Most of the ambitious climbers Mr. Slow had mentored previously were ready to leave the nest after four or five years. Arthur had been with the company for twice that time now—and while he was a valued and productive employee, Mr. Slow couldn't understand why he was still hanging around.

Had marriage and fatherhood slowed him down?

Was it the growth-challenged national economy?

What was he afraid of?

Success?

In truth, he supposed that Arthur had simply grown too comfortable in his surroundings. He made good money, ate good food—too much, Charlie Slow often thought to himself—and could do his job with ease. He was overconfident and felt there was nothing left to learn.

Charlie Slow was quite disturbed by these thoughts. Arthur had so much potential, but it was lying dormant. He deserved so much more—and so did his lovely wife. *That's it!* Slow decided. He had to do something. But what? Should he talk to Arthur? He wasn't sure a "pep talk" would do the trick. Maybe he should just fire him, forcing Arthur to move on? But that plan could backfire with dire consequences for Arthur's entire family.

Unsure which tactic to take, Slow turned to the one person he knew could advise him and would have Arthur's best interests at heart. He called on his old friend and Arthur's former boss, Jonathan Patient. Slow knew that Arthur kept in touch with Jonathan, and suspected that

Patient saw the same problems with Arthur that he did. Who better to help?

The two of them met for lunch, and after discussing the "Arthur problem," they hit upon the solution—one so obvious, they almost missed it.

Arthur was honestly offended when Mr. Slow said he wanted him to come in off the road one week every month and spend time with him . . . as his personal assistant. Arthur would accompany Mr. Slow on all his business trips, be beside him at every meeting, hear what he heard, see what he saw.

The only thing Arthur heard his boss say, however, was that he would be driving Mr. Slow from place to place.

Mr. Slow never said the word, but Arthur heard the word "chauffeur" ringing in his ears.

"I'll pay you for those weeks commensurate with what you would otherwise earn in sales commissions," Mr. Slow said. "But I think you and I would both benefit from working and traveling together. I want to know more about the marshmallow principle—and I might suggest you could learn a thing or two from me about running a business."

Arthur didn't like the idea one bit. *Not one little bit!* Go back to being a driver? He thought he had left those days behind once he learned and mastered the marshmallow principle.

Akilah agreed that it seemed an odd step on the corporate ladder, neither upward nor even lateral, but there was no denying that Mr. Slow thought highly of Arthur, especially after he guided Bryan Slow to college and proved himself to be SlowDown! Inc.'s number one salesman and customer service provider.

So Akilah, who now wanted more than anything for her husband to become the man she'd thought she'd married—confident and inventive—advised him to be patient and see this curveball through.

"Our income won't be affected," she said, kissing him on the lips for the first time in weeks, "so what's the harm?"

•   •   •

As it turned out, there were days when Arthur was glad to be off the road, but there were also many weeks when he was on a hot streak, when his mojo was working overtime, and he wanted nothing more than to keep milking it and stay out amongst his clients, building rapport and earning fat commissions.

Six months into this arrangement, Arthur had seen Mr. Slow give his standard motivational speech at least a hundred times to professional associations, chambers of commerce, and other civic groups.

One day Arthur told his boss, "Mr. Slow, no disrespect,

but don't you think I've been doing this personal assistant thing long enough? I've traveled with you so much and heard you so many times that I have memorized your speech word for word."

"What? You know my speech word for word? Are you sure about that?"

"I certainly am," Arthur said.

"Well, one day I'm going to test you," Mr. Slow said. "I hope you're not lying to me."

"No, no, of course not! Go on, test me, I can recite your speech right now if you'd like."

Mr. Slow looked at Arthur, shook his head slightly, and chuckled.

•   •   •

A month later, Arthur was again driving Mr. Slow to a talk. This time they were in New Jersey, on the way to an appearance before MBA candidates at Princeton University.

"Arthur, there's a McDonald's up ahead on the right. Stop in there for a moment, will you?"

Arthur, thinking they were going to have breakfast, smiled and nodded. Even though he'd had breakfast before he left the house this morning, he could always go for a little snack.

But when they got there, Mr. Slow got out of the car

and said, "Arthur, I'm going to the men's room. Come with me."

"Uh, sir?"

"Just follow me."

Once the restroom door closed, Mr. Slow started taking his clothes off.

"Mr. Slow," Arthur said, trying to make a joke, "that's *not* what you hired me for!"

"No, no, of course not!" he said, roaring with laughter. "No, today I am going to test you. They don't know me in Princeton, so *you're* going to do the speech."

"WHAT?!?"

Mr. Slow kept removing articles from his three-piece, finely hand-tailored suit and passed them over to his startled chauffeur.

"You're kidding, Mr. Slow, right? Come on, don't do this to me. I will happily tell you the speech back in the car, but I will not stand in front of strangers and recite *your* speech. That's ridiculous!"

"C'mon, my boy," Mr. Slow said. "You *said* you knew my speech. You're such a big shot that you think you can give my speech? Okay, you can do it today at Princeton University."

"I cannot do that. No way, sir."

Arthur was steadfast, determined not to budge.

"Well, if you won't give the speech, Arthur, you're fired."

Mr. Slow sighed heavily and started putting his pants back on.

"I'm fired?"

Arthur looked at his boss of the past decade for some sort of signal that this was all a gag, a big joke. But Mr. Slow wasn't laughing.

"Mr. Slow, please! I *need* this job. I cannot be fired."

Arthur realized he had no choice but to accept the challenge, uncertain whether Mr. Slow would actually fire him in the men's room of a New Jersey fast-food restaurant.

Arthur dressed as Mr. Slow; Mr. Slow became the chauffeur, carrying on the charade to the point of getting behind the wheel of the car and telling Arthur to sit in the back as a VIP passenger would.

Reaching the university auditorium, Mr. Slow took a seat in the back of the room and nodded to Arthur to take the long walk to the stage. Arthur shook hands with the assorted business school students present; they assumed he was Mr. Slow and while he never confirmed it, he didn't deny it, either. Arthur took a seat on the stage as the program got under way.

As his turn to speak drew closer, Arthur's heart was beating so fast he feared it might leap out of his chest. He had no trouble speaking to small groups, but before him were hundreds of graduate students and their professors. Why had he ever boasted that he could give Mr. Slow's speech?

"Ladies and gentlemen," the moderator said, "it's a pleasure to introduce, from SlowDown! Inc., chairman and founder, Charlie Slow."

Arthur went to the podium and began.

"Good evening. My name is Charlie Slow."

There was a profound silence in the auditorium. Arthur felt a wave of horror hit him. *They know!* he thought. *They know I'm not Mr. Slow! My career—no, my life!—is over!*

He took a deep breath and remembered it was confidence that put him in this position and he would need some measure of arrogance to survive the situation.

He started talking, one sentence leading into the next, forming paragraphs of shared knowledge, all presented by rote.

In the back of the auditorium, Arthur could see Mr. Slow—dressed as his chauffeur—motioning him onward . . . and smiling!

Arthur felt his familiar confidence returning and noticed the students and professors hanging on every word despite what he, personally, thought was a rough start. It was like Arthur had the lead in the school play, emphasizing his points with the same dramatic movements that Mr. Slow used.

Everything that Mr. Slow did, Arthur did—only faster. Two minutes faster overall, in fact.

When he reached the end of his prepared remarks, Arthur—as Mr. Slow—said, "Thank you," accepted a hearty round of applause, and made his way back to his seat.

The moderator returned to the microphone, looked back at Arthur, and said, "Okay, now we'll open the floor for questions."

Arthur thought he would lose consciousness. He knew the speech, but could hardly be expected to answer questions as his boss!

Oh, no!

"No questions," Arthur said. "I finished my speech—all done."

"I'm sorry, Mr. Slow," the moderator whispered, his hand covering the microphone, making it clear this was not an acceptable response. "At Princeton University, our MBA candidates always ask questions of our paid speakers. It was explicitly written in your contract . . . So please, ladies and gentlemen, any questions?"

The first hand went up and the moderator bid a young man to come forward to the microphone.

"Mr. Slow," he said, "you said that the skills needed to

sell low-priced items are much different than the skills you would need to sell high-priced items or high-priced services. Could you expound on that theory?"

Arthur wondered if anyone would notice him throwing up in the potted plant on the corner of the stage.

He did not even begin to know the answer to that question.

Or maybe he did, but it was nowhere in his thoughts right now. He wasn't even sure what his name was at this very moment. Was this something he knew? Could the audience see the sweat beading on his forehead? Did they hear his heart pounding in his chest? Was there any chance this was just a horrible, horrible dream after eating too many helpings of Akilah's Cuban mojo chicken?

There was silence throughout the room as people looked at Arthur, who himself looked for the nearest exit. *I have to get out of here. I don't know what to say or do.* He saw Mr. Slow's face, which had turned from pride to anxiety.

As he stared at Mr. Slow for relief, Arthur had a simple idea.

He looked at the person who asked the question and said, "Young man, with all due respect, that is such a stupid question that I will have my chauffeur answer it. Come here, Arthur." And with that he left the stage, his eyes begging Mr. Slow to save him.

3

A Growing Confidence Behind the Wheel

Arthur and Mr. Slow had quite a chuckle over Arthur's ingenious "save" at Princeton, and his performance convinced his boss that he was the quick, innovative man he was always thought to be. But Mr. Slow knew that Arthur needed to go from parroting Mr. Slow's remarks to believing in them—and believing in himself.

"Arthur, do not give anyone permission to make you feel inferior," Mr. Slow said.

"How do I do that?" Arthur asked. "Most days I feel extremely sure of myself, but sometimes I feel myself backsliding to a time when I didn't believe in myself."

"You have to keep your self-esteem in high gear," Mr. Slow said. "There are two ways to do this. One is with a physical cue. You know the famous experiments by the Russian psychophysiologist Ivan Petrovich Pavlov in which he would ring a bell while dangling meat in front of a hungry dog?"

"Of course."

"Well, Pavlov did it so many times that he conditioned the dogs to salivate at the sound of the bell without even showing the meat."

"So I'm a hungry dog?" Arthur asked, not sure where his boss was going with this.

"Well, yes . . . and no," Mr. Slow said. "A more modern example involves a sports psychologist, Ken Baum, who modified this idea when working with athletes. He taught them that performance cues such as the bell give permanence to an experience such as throwing a perfect fastball or scoring a beautiful layup. When his players were in a demanding situation, he'd advise them to use a word or a touch that would always take them back to a moment when they executed a move with precision and accuracy. Then he adapted these cues to businesspeople so they would touch their wrist or a belt buckle to take them to a place and time of perfect execution. Does that make sense?"

"I think so," Arthur said. "I think I may already do something like that when I'm closing a sale; I just never had a name for it before. When I feel it's time to push the client for a signature, I always rub my right earlobe before launching into my close."

"That's it, exactly!"

"That was easy, then. What's the second step?"

"Never allow *anyone* to put you down," Mr. Slow said. "Never allow *anyone* to say you're not good enough. Never allow *anyone* to say that you're going to fail because, in his or her mind, you are not up to par or not good enough. Never give that permission to *anyone* else."

Mr. Slow shared with Arthur a story he had heard in his early days as a public speaker. It had as much to do with confidence as anything and he thought hearing it might help Arthur stop thinking of himself as Mr. P's former chauffeur and start seeing himself as a smart, independent man in his own right. It was a story about an ambitious young Hispanic motivational speaker and trainer for whom English was then a distant second language.

Based in Miami, he only gave speeches in Spanish to Latino audiences. Although he spoke English, he lacked enough confidence to consider selling himself to potential English-speaking audiences.

One day in the mid-1980s, he and his business partner were in Puerto Rico, watching TV. Henry Kissinger was on the news, giving his opinion on a political incident.

Kissinger, a native of Fürth, Germany, had managed to rise through government and private policy ranks to become the fifty-sixth Secretary of State of the United States, serving from 1973 to 1977 under two presidents, Richard M. Nixon and Gerald Ford. This despite bearing a remarkably thick German accent that he never even tried to shake.

"Felipe," his partner said, "look at *that* guy. *He* has an accent. But everyone in the world seems to understand what he is saying. If he can do it, why can't you?"

Felipe got the point, but it wasn't enough to overcome the embarrassment his English brought him in public.

Some months later, Felipe was invited to train a group of Hispanic Realtors. They all spoke Spanish, but Felipe didn't know anything about real estate. The man hiring him said, "Don't worry, you don't have to know anything about real estate. All you have to do is talk about psychology, motivation, and self-discipline—the usual subjects that you discuss."

Felipe agreed and was hired to do eight Saturday sessions of eight hours each—sixty-four hours total—for a fee of $1,500. But he still felt it important to know something about real estate before speaking to this professional association. He saw in the newspaper that the president of AAAA-Best Home Sales would be doing a public seminar on real estate sales and he made a reservation to attend. Felipe took voluminous notes, absorbing as much industry information as he could.

At the end of the session—which was entirely in English, it must be noted—the president of AAAA-Best Home Sales handed out index cards and asked everyone in the audience to write down their name, phone number, and a sentence about why they came. Most people in attendance were there to learn real estate, possibly to change careers. But Felipe? He was there to gain at least a superficial understanding of the real estate business so he could give a session to the speaker's competitor! Stating that didn't seem prudent—or respectful—so instead, Felipe wrote, "It was a great session. I really enjoyed it. You've got wonderful knowledge that I will be able to use. By the way, if you ever need a speaker, I'm the best motivational speaker in the U.S.!"

Felipe showed the woman sitting next to him what he wrote, thinking it would impress her. It did.

"Oh, my God," she said. "That's great."

Having impressed the woman, Felipe collected her phone number and bid her and the session farewell.

A few days later, Felipe received a phone call.

"Hello," a woman's voice said, "I'd like to talk to Felipe."

"This is Felipe," he said.

"This is Anne Marie. You sat next to me at the real estate seminar. Remember?"

Felipe said he did.

"I work for the president of AAAA-Best Home Sales. He would like to have lunch with 'the best motivational speaker in the U.S.'"

Felipe almost said, *Who the hell is that?* but then he remembered the little stunt he'd pulled to impress a girl at the end of the seminar. He thought about saying, *I'm terribly sorry but I'm on vacation . . . for the next two years!* But he decided to face the music and take his lumps for being so arrogant in his note.

"I'd love to have lunch with him," he said politely, and they set a date.

Felipe went that day with the intention of buying his host's lunch and apologizing for being there under false pretenses.

But nothing went as Felipe expected.

"You're an expert," the president of AAAA-Best Home Sales said. "So please, tell me, what did I do right? What did I do wrong? Can you provide me with some constructive criticism of my speech?"

"Oh, no. No!" Felipe said. "You were wonderful! I loved it. I really had a good time."

"No, no, no," the man said. "Tell me what I can do better. Tell me what improvements I can make." He was quite insistent.

Although Felipe had never given a single speech in English, he had given hundreds in Spanish. He knew his business, whatever language it was delivered in.

"You really want to know?" Felipe asked again, just to be sure before launching into a critique that could immediately alienate this powerful American businessman.

"Yes, please! I *do* want to know."

He took out a pad and, as Felipe started talking, started taking notes.

"Okay, first of all, when you discuss point A, don't show slides that tip off points B, C, D, and E. Just show point A, develop it, talk about it, and *then* move on to point B. Discuss it thoroughly and only then should you show point B to the audience. Because if you unveil your five principles in a single slide, people will get distracted and stop paying attention to what you're saying. They'll think they already know all they need to know from you."

"That's a great idea," he said.

"Let's talk about something else," Felipe continued.

"When you're speaking to a large audience like you did, you have to move around and look at everyone in the audience. You were only looking at one side, so the rest of the group felt alienated. You looked steadily at people on your left side, so the middle and the right did not feel engaged in the conference."

"Another good point!"

"One more thing," Felipe said.

"Yes . . . ?"

"You are scared to death of speaking in public. Am I right?"

There was a terrible, intimidating silence at the table. The man looked hard at Felipe, then abruptly relaxed his expression.

"How could you tell?" he asked, lowering his eyes.

"When you got to the lectern, you held on to it like you were holding on for dear life," Felipe said. "I could see your white knuckles. I could hear your voice trembling."

"You're right," he said. "I hate it, absolutely hate it, but if I don't do it my company will go under. I need to convince Realtors to adopt the AAAA-Best Home Sales name and best practices and to do that, I have to go all over the United States."

"In that case, here's one more tip that may help you—and your audience—feel more at ease. When you start speaking, look into a single pair of eyes. Choose someone in the middle of the room. Look at that person and speak to him or her as if there is no one else in the audience. Then look to your left and pick a second person to address for five seconds, and then do the same on your right. Pretty soon you're going to be shifting your gaze all over the auditorium, all the while only looking at one person at a time. No one will know but you. When you look into one pair of eyes, people think you're looking at the whole group in that direction, but you will feel like you are really doing a one-on-one and not talking to three hundred people."

"That is wonderful," he said, absorbing what Felipe had said. "Tell me something else: How did you become the best motivational speaker in the U.S.?"

Caught! Felipe knew he had to tell this kind gentleman the truth. But he decided to at least do it with humor.

"I learned at Harvard. Harvard University," Felipe said.

"You went to Harvard?"

"No, no, no. I didn't *go* to Harvard. I worked in the office of a Harvard business professor who *I* thought was the best motivational speaker in the U.S."

"So he taught you?"

"Not exactly. I heard him rehearsing the same speech over and over again, at least once or twice a week for months. I thought that if I memorized this speech by the best motivational speaker in the U.S., that would make me the best motivational speaker in the U.S. because I said exactly what the professor said."

"And it worked?"

"Yes—as long as I gave the speech in my native language, Spanish. I developed a following of my own among Hispanic business leaders and eventually left the professor's employ and struck out on my own. And now *I* am the best motivational speaker in the U.S.!"

Felipe said it in such a way that both men laughed. The president of AAAA-Best Home Sales knew now it was a boast, one on which Felipe never dreamed he would be challenged.

The president of AAAA-Best Home Sales studied Felipe for a moment, then reached into his briefcase under the table.

"I have another big conference in two months," he said. "There will be seven hundred people there. There is another speaker I am considering, but I would love to give you the chance to make a presentation. However, I don't think I can risk it based on today's lunch alone."

Felipe was confused . . . and disappointed. Was his big break slipping away from him because of a moment's overconfidence and arrogance?

"I'll tell you what," the president said. "You come to my

headquarters office next week in Tampa and give a two-hour motivational presentation to my people—my managers, my customer service people, my secretary, and all the rest. If they like what you do and are convinced you're *that* good, I'll hire you for the big one."

"Wow," Felipe said, "that's very generous of you. And how much would I get paid if I get the job?"

"Fifteen hundred dollars."

At that point in Felipe's career, he had to make eight, eight-hour presentations on consecutive Saturdays to make as much as the president of AAAA-Best Home Sales proposed to pay him for a *single* session. In other words, to earn $1,500 for a two-hour speech versus $1,500 for sixty-four hours of work. Quite a difference!

It also brought to the fore the difference between what the Latin market and the American market could pay him.

"I think I can do it for that price," Felipe said. "In fact, I would love to do it."

The AAAA-Best Home Sales staff loved Felipe—in English and with an accent!—and he earned a shot at the big time. Speaking to an audience of seven hundred led to a six-month contract with AAAA-Best Home Sales that had him traveling every Saturday to a different AAAA-Best Home Sales office in Florida.

When Mr. Slow finished telling the story, Arthur let out

a low, long whistle as he exhaled. He suddenly knew where his experiences, first with Mr. P and now with the Slow family, had led him. He was like that Hispanic motivational speaker who worked for the Harvard professor.

He also understood, for the first time, that in life we make up our own obstacles. We sometimes lack faith in ourselves. We have low self-esteem and we do not try for what we want because we think we're not going to be good enough. Hearing Felipe's story of ambition and overcoming obstacles inspired him in ways nothing previously had accomplished. The parallels to his own life—substituting linguistic challenges for the financial hardships Arthur had overcome—made a deep impression. It taught Arthur a very important lesson.

Arthur shared all this with Mr. Slow, who smiled approvingly. He always knew Arthur had it within himself to grow and mature; he just didn't know when it would happen.

"Oh, and Arthur?"

"Yes, Mr. Slow?"

"There is a little more to Felipe's story. Do you want to hear it?"

"Of course! Please!"

As it happened, Felipe ran into the same real estate executive several years later, by which point he had retired from the business. They gave each other a hug and agreed to meet later for a drink to reminisce. Felipe appreciated the unexpected opportunity to thank him for having hired him and jump-starting his career as an English language motivational speaker.

"I will always hold a very special place in my heart for you because you gave me faith, you trusted me," Felipe said. "If you need anything in life, you can count on me. I will help you out with anything you need. But there is *one* condition."

"Thank you, Felipe," he said. "But wait—what's the condition?"

"You never told me the name of the other speaker you were considering for that first meeting when you ultimately hired me. Instead of hiring him, you gave me the chance of a lifetime. But over the years I always wondered: Who was that guy?"

"I never told you?"

"No, no," Felipe said, "you never told me."

"I was prepared to hire Norman Vincent Peale, the number one speaker in the nation."

Felipe gasped.

"But I, too, have to confess something," the retired businessman said.

"You? What? What do you have to confess?"

"You won't get mad?"

"Of course not. You gave me the biggest break in my life!"

"I paid you *half* of what I was going to pay him."

The story taught Felipe—and, a generation later, Arthur—a very important lesson: that everyone has a chance.

"The only person that can knock you out of the running," Mr. Slow said, "is yourself."

4

A Test of Grit

Since leaving Mr. P's employ, Arthur regularly met with him for a coffee or lunch. Every two months or so, the two would get together to discuss business challenges, life challenges, and simply to catch up. But Arthur was surprised when they met one day and Mr. P asked Arthur to take a pair of personality tests designed to help people identify their motives, values, and preferences. These tests also highlighted potential career derailing tendencies—also called shadows—that include eleven patterns of behavior that impede work relationships, hinder productivity, or limit overall career potential.

In the clinical world, these dysfunctional characteristics are called borderline, paranoid, avoidant, schizoid, passive-aggressive, narcissistic, antisocial, histrionic, schizotypal, obsessive-compulsive, and dependent.

In a labor market, these items would be characterized as excitable, skeptical, cautious, reserved, leisurely, bold, mischievous, colorful, imaginative, diligent, and dutiful.

The test was administered at Jonathan Patient's office and Mr. P discussed the results with his protégé.

"The counterproductive behaviors the tests reveal actually arise from strengths that you might have. Let's say that I am extremely self-confident. That's my strength; that's what gets me ahead, that is what gets me promoted in the company, and that's what gets me noticed.

"But if I take self-confidence to a high degree," he continued, "it becomes a weakness because I become arrogant. All of these counter behaviors arise from a strength overdone or overplayed or are due to falling short on a necessary behavior. Context will ultimately determine if a characteristic is favorable or unfavorable, advantageous or disadvantageous.

"Arthur, you're a really self-confident fellow. But when you're under pressure to perform, you often become arrogant. You think you know all the answers because you are confident . . . sometimes beyond rationality. 'Don't bring me ideas. Don't tell me what to do. I don't and won't listen'—and that's how you sometimes have found yourself skidding downhill. That's how you will lose a job—or a person—you love and will never have seen it coming."

Mr. P told Arthur the cautionary tale of the first woman CEO at one of America's biggest blue-chip corporations. Sadly, that same self-confidence manifested itself as arrogance when times turned tough and ultimately sped her downfall. She didn't listen to her board of directors or anyone in her inner circle; she didn't see the warning signs right in front of her. *I know how things should be done around here! I got here my way. I know how to succeed. Don't tell me stuff that I don't need to know!*

"Like this woman," Mr. P told Arthur, "you are bold, assertive, and energetic. You come across as confident, ambitious, and visionary, often unafraid of failure or rejection.

"On the other hand, when those strengths are overused or overemphasized during those times when you are under pressure, you become impulsive, self-promoting, unresponsive to negative feedback, too competitive and demanding. This may be why you drive Akilah crazy at times! You, my young friend, also tend to overestimate your talents and accomplishments, ignore shortcomings, and blame your mistakes on others.

"Yes, Arthur, you do make an excellent first impression,"

he added. "But when you are under lots of stress or pressure, you can be hard to work with because you feel that you deserve special treatment. You tend to ignore constructive criticism and you intimidate your subordinates. All of this combined makes it hard to build loyalty and develop teamwork among your employees."

Arthur's first instinct was to defend himself, but that defensiveness was soon replaced by shame and embarrassment.

"Arthur, I don't say these things to belittle you. My intent is not to make you feel bad, but give you an invaluable tool—self-knowledge. The people around you see these things and form impressions and opinions about you based on them. At home, Akilah sees them. So do the twins. On the job, from supervisors to direct reports, your coworkers see them. Only *you* don't.

"You want to know what your reputation is under normal conditions, and you want to know what your reputation is under stress. Your 'shadow' shows up when you are under stress, bored or when anxiety is present."

Arthur was not the first person Mr. P had advised to take the personality test. He told Arthur about a CEO he knew who, under pressure, became so cautious that he grew incapable of making key decisions. He *thought* he made decisions when they had to be made, but the test results conclusively showed him that when he was under extreme stress or pressure, he became paralyzed: *I will not make important decisions that could affect the company because we could go bankrupt if I make the wrong decisions.*

By discovering this about himself, he was able to consciously get help in crises. Now—without announcing this characteristic about himself—he creates dialogues with the people around him and they help him stride more wisely through possible scenarios and decisions. *You're right,* he says. *We have to move on this.*

"In your case, Arthur, I don't believe you even know that your self-confidence and boldness manifest as counterproductive behavior at times."

Arthur felt utterly dejected. "I thought I was acting confidently," he said. "I thought that was a plus; I thought people admired that. But if I'm at a level where I'm arrogant, that's not good. Arrogance will bring down my credibility and that, in turn, will destroy my relationship with my people. I hated hearing it but I'm so glad you told me."

But Mr. P wasn't done yet. He introduced Arthur to an article that came out in the *Journal of Personality and Social Psychology* that spoke about researchers from the University of Pennsylvania. In this study, Dr. Angela Duckworth and her colleagues took the original marshmallow principle a step further.

"First of all," Mr. P said, "Dr. Duckworth says that the marshmallow principle is not the whole story. It's true. They found that there is another factor that plays a part in how successful people are going to be. They isolated two qualities that are good predictors of success. One of them is the tendency to stick with what you are doing and not abandon the task for mere changeability or because you get bored. Not seeking something because of novelty. Not looking for a change.

"The second one is perseverance, tenacity, doggedness; in other words, not giving up or abandoning tasks in the face of obstacles. Dr. Duckworth posited that people who accomplish great things often combine a passion for a single mission with unswerving dedication to achieving that mission, whatever the obstacles and however long it might take. And then Dr. Duckworth boiled these two characteristics down to a quality she called 'grit,' which she defined as the perseverance and passion for a long-term goal."

"It's a very interesting concept," Mr. P said.

"It has a lot to do with ambition. People with a high level of ambition tend to be leaderlike, energetic, driven, competitive and focused on achieving results which will lead to success. They will also take initiative, be persistent when completing a task, and are eager to advance in their own business or in any organization for which they work. There is no doubt that these individuals are self-confident and have a knack for focusing on whatever they want and not letting go until they get it. Some, such as Steve Jobs, take it a step further. Whatever he was interested in, he would take to sometimes irrational extremes. When he decided that something had to happen, by golly, he stuck to it until it happened. But that step has its risks.

"Jobs had a friend named Robert Friedland who introduced him to the 'reality distortion field' concept. The reality distortion field is akin to what the Israeli-American psychologist and 2002 Nobel Prize winner in Economic Sciences, Daniel Kahneman, calls a 'pervasive optimistic bias.' He said, 'Most of us view the world as more benign than it really is, our own attributes as more favorable than they truly are and the goals we adopt as more achievable than they are likely to be.'

"Let me give you an example: Less than forty percent of small businesses don't go bankrupt in our country and yet in a survey, more than eighty percent of small business owners estimated their chance to succeed at seventy percent and a third of them went so far as to put it at one hundred percent.

"There is no doubt that one of the benefits of being extremely optimistic is that you will be more persistent in overcoming any obstacles that get in your way, but I must warn you that it could backfire because it can make you blind to symptoms that indicate imminent failure and that the best course of action is to cut your losses and get out of the business."

Being overly optimistic to the point of distorting reality can lead a person to take dangerous and unnecessary risks such as the ones that Steve Jobs took.

There was one reality distortion field that dear Mr. Jobs could not bring to its knees: cancer.

He was diagnosed in 2003 with pancreatic cancer, which likely would have been treatable with surgery. In fact, according to Walter Isaacson, Jobs's biographer, when the surgeons diagnosed it, they were happy because they had found the cancer in time for him to be totally cured. But, what happened? Jobs refused the surgery to remove the tumor. Isaacson quoted him as saying, "I really didn't want them to open up my body, so I tried to see if a few other things would work." What did he do? Drink lots of carrot and fruit juices; fast for days; try acupuncture, hydrotherapy, vegan diets, and herbal remedies; and he even had his bowel cleansed several times. For goodness' sake, this intelligent man went to a psychic to find a cure for his cancer! How in the world can that be possible?

When you get used to distorting reality the way Steve

Jobs did for so long—in fact, so successfully that he revolutionized six industries: tablet computing, personal computers, digital music, animated films, cell phones, and digital publishing—you start thinking that you are infallible, and that is dangerous. That little business he started in his parents' garage became the world's most valuable company and he changed the world. There is no doubt that to that end, his reality distortion field served him well but in the end, it may have killed him.

Out of this magnificent—some would say heroic—life, one big lesson emerged: Reality must take precedence over uncontrolled optimism, because in the final analysis, nature can't be distorted.

"One of the people I admired the most over the years was Viktor Frankl, who wrote *Man's Search for Meaning*," Mr. P said. "In that book, he says that we have control over how we respond to what happens to us. I daresay that often we actually don't. Emotions happen to us and even though Wayne Dyer said that emotions come from thoughts and if we can control thoughts we obviously can control emotions, I really don't agree with him one hundred percent. For example, look at your watch now: For fifteen seconds, do not think about an elephant. *Come on, don't think about the elephant.* Try again—for fifteen seconds don't think about an elephant. What happened? You can't stop think-ing about an elephant, so you can't control your thoughts or at least you don't know how to control them.

"Emotion usually wins the battle with intellect in de-termining behavior, unless you have been endowed with an iron will.

"But Viktor wasn't totally wrong, either," he continued. "Though total control over our response to negative events may evade us, influence over it might not. If we can't change our emotional behavior by a strong will, we can at least increase the likelihood that we react constructively by de-veloping something psychologists call 'personality hardi-ness': the capacity to survive and even prosper under demanding conditions.

"Personality hardiness, contrary to what people think, isn't something with which only a few of us, the lucky ones, were born with, but rather something we can all, with hard work, develop. You develop personality hardiness by making an effort to interpret change as normal, inevitable, and as an inspiring, positive challenge, not as a threat. You must view your life as meaningful, your problems as opportuni-ties, and the future as an adventure."

5

A Momentous Decision

Arthur, the man who once thought he knew it all, was learning so much from Mr. Slow and Mr. P. He eagerly absorbed all the lessons they taught him, and gradually he felt himself transform and grow.

Arthur woke up one morning and realized what a lucky man he was, indeed. Loving wife, two healthy children, and two business mentors who believed in his ability to succeed against whatever obstacles came his way. He finally knew what he had to do, and he had the self-confidence to do it.

He invited Mr. P and Mr. Slow to join him and Akilah for dinner at her restaurant, Just Ask. All he told them in advance was that he wanted to talk about the future, but both men had an inkling of what was coming.

A babysitter was arranged for the twins and Akilah went to work on a special menu for the dinner party.

As for Arthur, he had been mentally preparing for this moment for months, mustering the confidence to take the next step in his life—and to do so without the self-defeating arrogance Mr. P had warned him about. Arthur need not look to anyone's life but his own to be reminded how unchecked arrogance could derail one's goals.

When he was on the verge of graduating college, Arthur had bragged to his circle of friends about the $100,000 job he'd already landed. The job part was true—working for Mr. Slow's company, SlowDown! Inc.—but the salary was a bit of an illusion. The figure was based upon *anticipated* sales commissions, not salary. After a minimal draw to get him started, Arthur would have to earn every penny as a salesman. He confused the job's potential with reality. Unfortunately, the former chauffeur who had learned to save his "marshmallows" to pay for college had already spent thousands of dollars in advance, assuming an expensive new lifestyle that put him in a heap of debt from the day he started work.

Of course, even arrogance had its rewards: Coming down to earth had led him to fall in love with Akilah and all the good things that came with her, including the twins, Orly and Justin.

So here he waited, at yet another big fork in the road, determined, as Yogi Berra might have advised, to take it.

The day began as so many in South Florida did: The sun shone bright and made everything under it seem fresh and renewed. Arthur and Akilah awoke facing one another, shared a smile, embraced, and, *well . . .* you don't need to know all the details of their lives, do you?

Arthur took the children to school so Akilah could make an early start at the restaurant, preparing for the evening's special guests. At the office, Arthur merrily breezed through his paperwork and call sheets, taking great pleasure in each task as if it might be the last time he performed it.

(That is what is called foreshadowing.)

By the time evening came, Arthur had rehearsed his announcement to Mr. P and Mr. Slow so many times that he could now do it in his sleep. Appropriate, since last night he'd dreamed of how every bit of dinner tasted, how lovely Akilah looked in the restaurant's romantic lighting, and how his mentors hung on to and approved his every word.

Reality, however, had a way of turning even the most perfect dream into a nightmare in which nobody gets out alive.

Arthur had been so focused on his endgame that he forgot a few important steps along the way, starting with picking up the children after school. On a normal day, Akilah took a break from work and brought them back to the restaurant to do homework and play with her executive chef's kids. The executive chef's kids were at the restaurant, but an hour after her own twins were due, Akilah became worried. She called Arthur but there was no answer on his phone. She called the school and discovered the children were still waiting outside to be picked up.

Akilah dropped what she was doing and collected her children. They were more concerned about Daddy than upset at having to wait. But Akilah was just angry. How typical of Arthur to get so caught up in his work that he'd forget his own children.

Returning to the restaurant and rewarding the twins' patience with double servings of their favorite ice cream, she called the office at SlowDown! Inc. only to discover Arthur had already left for the day, saying he had some "special errands" to run.

Akilah waited for her husband to check in.

The longer it took, the more anger was replaced with worry. Where could he be? Had something bad happened? Why hadn't Arthur or someone—the police, a hospital— called her?

She tried to focus on work and preparations for the big dinner, but her anxieties got the best of her. By five P.M., she turned over the final preparations to her executive chef and got back in her car and went looking for Arthur.

If he wasn't at work and he wasn't in a car accident and he hadn't been kidnapped, where was Arthur?

Suddenly, she knew.

Akilah turned the car around and drove . . . *home.*

Sure enough, she found her husband in their spare bedroom, staring out the window . . . daydreaming. Again.

"Hello, Arthur," she said, barely restraining her bubbling anger.

"Akilah! Hi! *Um* . . . what are you doing home at this hour?"

"Oh, I forgot a couple things and wondered if I left them here," she said, her sarcasm lost on her husband, who was still in la-la land.

"What did you forget, dear?"

"Your children."

"The children? *Wha*—?"

Suddenly, Arthur's face turned ashen. His daydream of being his own boss and creating a million-dollar empire from a home office exploded in his brain.

"I screwed up," he said quietly.

"Not the words I would have used, but yes," Akilah said.

"I'm so, so sorry."

"'Sorry' doesn't cover it today, Arthur. If this family is going to count on you to leave your job and turn our lives upside down and inside out, we have to be able to count on you to handle at least a few insignificant details—such as picking up our kids from school and caring enough to wonder where they are when school ends. What is *wrong* with you?"

"I, *er . . . um . . .*"

"Never mind. Right now, you go to the restaurant, pick up the children, and take them to the babysitter's house."

"Where will you be?"

"I'm going to take a long shower and try to remember why I didn't take all the money I saved from waitressing years ago and just go on a bender to Las Vegas instead of committing the best years of my life to you. And maybe, just maybe, I'll be at the restaurant at seven thirty P.M. to make final preparations for dinner. You'll just have to wait there and wonder what I will choose to do."

Arthur looked at his wife, this delectable, brilliant woman who essentially chose him so many years ago, and felt himself deflate. She was right; he had gone beyond screwing up. Once more he had allowed himself to put his ambitions and business desires before all else in his life, endangering his children and angering and bewildering his wife.

"I'm sorry, Akilah," he said. "I'll do whatever you need from me. I do love you. And I hope you'll be there tonight. I need you more than anything else."

As Arthur left, a wounded puppy dog, Akilah felt a momentary pang of regret for taking him down a few pegs. Tonight might be the biggest night of his life yet and he needed to be at his best and brightest, what his college friends would have now updated to call "The Million-Dollar Man." But he was still just a man and one for whom this was not his first slip off the responsibility bus.

Akilah did show up for dinner that night—just moments ahead of Mr. P and Mr. Slow to keep her husband guessing—and she looked like a movie star. In fact, if Mr. P and Mr. Slow could have read each other's thoughts when she walked into the restaurant's main dining room, they would have laughed at sharing a single thought: "I wonder if I should have invested my time and energy in *her* rather than Arthur?" She looked that good and exuded that much charisma and sense of accomplishment.

Nothing passed between Arthur and Akilah to suggest anything was amiss, although Arthur did hesitate a few times in speaking to his wife.

When dinner was done and everyone had marveled at what a wonderful restaurateur Akilah had become, Arthur stood and thanked his wife, first for a delicious meal and second for standing by him through the good and the bad. Then he thanked his guests for taking time from their busy schedules to join them.

"As you all know, I was a bit of a late bloomer in life," Arthur began. "At a time when my high school friends were already well along in their careers and personal lives, I was a bit adrift. I was a poor chauffeur, spending every penny I earned from Mr. P, living from paycheck to paycheck with nothing to show for my labors.

"One day, Mr. P explained the marshmallow theory to me, how saving a marshmallow today, then two the next day, and so on, could create a wealth of marshmallows. I put the theory to the test and soon had more marshmallows than I ever dreamed.

"When I switched from collecting marshmallows to dollars, my entire life changed. I saved enough to put myself through college, although Mr. P gave me a good chunk of money to get me started. Then I met and fell in love with Akilah and cultivated a wonderful group of new friends. After graduating, I was hired for a dream job at SlowDown! Inc. and—after an admittedly bumpy start—I have done extremely well under Mr. Slow's tutelage.

"Over the years Akilah and I have continued to apply the major tenets of the marshmallow theory to our lives, saving as much as we could and making hopefully wise choices about how to live our lives and raise our two beautiful, healthy children.

"Tonight, I've reached one more of those decision points and I invited you here so I could share my choice with those closest to me."

"Somehow," Akilah said, "I don't think this is going to be as big a surprise as Arthur hoped, looking at the smiles on your faces."

Mr. P and Mr. Slow were beaming. Arthur just noticed it and he flushed.

"You already know?" he asked.

Mr. Slow looked at Mr. P and nodded.

"Let's just say we have our suspicions, Arthur," Mr. P said, grinning. "But please, proceed!"

Arthur laughed.

"Then I guess this is Miami's worst-kept secret: I've decided to strike out on my own as a professional business coach and motivational speaker, following in both of your footsteps. I hope you'll approve?"

Mr. P was first. He stood up, looked from Arthur to Akilah, then back to Arthur. He started clapping his hands together. Mr. Slow stood beside him and followed suit.

"We just have one question, Arthur," Mr. Slow said.

"Yes, sir?"

"What took you so long?"

Everyone laughed and several toasts were made. Akilah's executive chef rolled out a large sheet cake on which tiny marshmallows spelled out "Best of Luck, Arthur and Akilah!" (It was only supposed to say "Arthur," but when Akilah disappeared that afternoon, her sous chef took a few liberties with the inscription.)

Mr. P and Mr. Slow shook Arthur's hand to convey their approval and endorsement.

Akilah slipped behind her husband and whispered in his ear, "Don't screw this up."

He turned to say something to her, but she was gone.

6

Back to the Answer Man

A few lucky breaks and a key introduction of Arthur to a major client of Mr. P's set his new solo venture on the fast track.

The biggest opportunity of them all? An invitation to make a presentation at the legendary TED Conference.[1] TED—which began in 1984 as a nonprofit annual event devoted to bringing together the best new ideas in technology, entertainment, and design—grew exponentially in the Internet era and began reaching its largest audience ever

[1] To learn more about the TED Talks, visit www.TED.com.

in the twenty-first century when presentations were posted online via YouTube.

Being invited to present at TED was an unexpected thrill for Arthur, and that helped him leap ahead of his competition. He booked multiple speaking engagements from enthusiastic attendees in the audience the very day of his ten-minute presentation, but once the video hit the World Wide Web, interest in his life's pursuit went global. His website, DontEatTheMarshmallow.com, went from a few hundred visitors a day to as many as ten thousand per day.

As he'd hoped, Arthur's message of self-confidence, mindful savings, and well-being—which he marketed as "The Marshmallow Effect"—was an immediate hit in both business circles and among individuals seeking a sustaining approach to career and relationships. Men and women alike immediately grasped the simple tenets of logic in his presentation and its application to their lives.

Future bookings increased thanks largely to positive word of mouth, social media postings by pleased attendees, and Arthur's sheer commitment to sharing what he himself had learned working for Mr. P and Mr. Slow.

Start-up expenses were covered during his first year on his own and in year two Arthur began to see just how profitable his new career independence could be. He moved his operation from a spare room in the family's condominium to a small office on Brickell Avenue—Miami's official address for businesses that have arrived. The address was more impressive than the space itself, he thought, but who cared?

But while business boomed, the marital uneasiness that had come to the surface the night of Arthur's big dinner announcement persisted.

Arthur and Akilah continued to clash. Their bad moments together were starting to outnumber the good and it was all she could do to keep up the appearance of harmony in front of the children. Akilah was frustrated with her husband and her emotions could not possibly stay in check forever.

In practice, Akilah was more attuned to The Marshmallow Effect than its greatest public proponent—her husband.

Arthur, who had remained a bachelor many years after most of his contemporaries had married and raised families, was a loving husband and father but couldn't shake all of his former single man habits. He was accustomed to making decisions for himself, following the practices taught to him while working as a chauffeur for Mr. P. But living the marshmallow life and sticking with the program while making room for the needs and desires of others was proving a serious challenge.

He wanted to be the best man he could be for Akilah and the kids, he really did, but he didn't always know how.

Arthur proved himself a Master of the Universe in business, but came up short in his responsibilities to his family. He daydreamed too much, forgetting moments that were important to those who loved him.

In many ways, Arthur began to feel he was a fraud. He was telling people all over the world how to improve their lives, but he could no longer make things right in his own.

Realizing that his long devotion to marshmallow logic hadn't prepared him for making decisions with a partner, he decided it was time to go back to the source, the man who'd straightened him out more than once before when he'd gone off the tracks, the one individual who never seemed to have a bad day or say the wrong word to anyone.

Arthur called upon his mentor, Jonathan Patient, for guidance. If anyone could point out his missteps and errors of judgment, it was Mr. P. For the last several years, Mr. P had always been there when Arthur stumbled; surely he would know what Arthur should do.

*   *   *

"Hello, Arthur!" Jonathan Patient said, coming out of the house to greet his mentee as he climbed the steps of his palatial home.

"Hello, Mr. P . . . *er*, Jonathan!" Arthur said. Even after all these years, his respect for Jonathan Patient was so great and ingrained that he still felt the need to address him as "Mister."

"I was so happy to get your call. We don't seem to talk as often as we did before you started your own business," Mr. P said, chuckling.

Quietly, Arthur said, "My wife isn't talking to me as often as she did before I started my own business, either."

Mr. P stopped in his tracks.

"I'm sorry, Arthur, it must be my hearing. Did you say something about your wife?"

"I did, actually," Arthur admitted. "That's why I'm here. Akilah has been extremely unhappy with me, Jonathan. She can barely say two words to me anymore without getting mad. It's making life very difficult in our house."

"That doesn't sound like the Akilah I know, Arthur. Has she told you why she's upset?"

"Not really."

"No? It just started out of thin air?"

"Well . . ."

Jonathan looked at Arthur the way a father would when his son hits a baseball through a glass window and is waiting for the boy to admit what they both know he did and for which he needs to accept responsibility.

"Well . . . ?"

"She says I'm not paying enough attention to her and

the kids. That sometimes I act like they don't even exist and that I do whatever I want, whenever I want. That I make her count pennies while I'm spending thousands on myself and my business. That I take her business—the restaurant—for granted as a profit center that I exploit for my own purposes. And that it's like I'm not there, even when I am."

"I see."

"You do?"

"Let's just say it's not an experience with which I am unfamiliar, Arthur."

"You know someone else who has been through this, Mr. P?"

"Actually I do," Jonathan said.

"What did *he* do? How did he make it better? I love Akilah and the kids—you *know* that. *She* knows that. I just can't seem to say or do the right thing—ever."

Jonathan was silent for a moment, absorbing the younger man's pain and heartbreak. But for the first time in their long relationship, he was about to disappoint Arthur.

"Arthur . . ."

"Yes, Mr. . . . Jonathan? What did your friend do?"

"It wasn't a friend of mine who found himself on your path, Arthur."

"No?" Arthur was confused. Who could Mr. P be thinking of?

Both men were silent. Arthur looked into Jonathan Patient's eyes and suddenly, he knew. He couldn't believe it could be true.

"You, Jonathan?"

Jonathan nodded.

"We've never talked much about what I was like at your age, Arthur," the older man said. "And you've never wondered—or at least asked—about my personal life. But I wasn't always the way you know me. I had my own mountains to climb, my own bad habits to break."

"I always thought you were . . ."

"What, Arthur?"

". . . perfect."

The tense moment was broken as Jonathan laughed heartily.

"Perfect? Me?" He laughed some more. "Couldn't be further from the truth."

"But . . ."

"Arthur, no one wants to discover their idols are made of straw, and no single person is totally perfect or imperfect. I have my flaws, just as you do, just as Akilah does, just as everyone we know does. You just chose not to see mine because you needed someone to inspire and guide you. And I, in turn, did my best over the years to insulate you from my imperfections so as not to damage your image of me."

"Are you saying that you went through what I am dealing with?"

"That's exactly what I'm saying. In some way, virtually every married person you'll ever meet experiences these types of relationship pains. It comes from being at close quarters for long periods of time, dealing together and separately with everything the world throws at a person. We either grow together or we grow apart."

"That's great!" Arthur said.

"Excuse me, Arthur?"

"I'm sorry, Mr. P. I didn't mean it was great you went through hell—well, maybe I did. Because since you've been there, you can show me the way out!"

"Not this time, Arthur."

"What? Why not?"

"Because I didn't make the right choices when I had the chance. That's why, despite my millions and successes in business, I live alone."

"You were married?"

"Absolutely."

"Kids?"

Arthur wasn't sure he wanted to hear a "yes" to that question and regretted even asking. He had never seen photographs of children in Mr. P's house.

"Two," Mr. P said.

"But . . ."

"Look, Arthur," Jonathan said, his voice taking on a tone Arthur had never heard before. And there was a sadness in Jonathan Patient's eyes that he had never seen. "There is a lot about me that you don't know, a lot that might surprise you."

"But . . ."

"You're not going to learn about those things from me. Not now, at least. There is someone I think you need to meet. You have had me for the last several years; I'm going to send you to my . . . well, *my* Mr. P, so to speak."

"*Your* Mr. P?"

The very idea that Jonathan ever needed someone to help guide *his* life was completely foreign to the truths Arthur always held dear about Mr. P. He always took for granted that Jonathan was perfectly formed in the womb and always made the right moves and had all the answers to life's questions.

There had been times over the years when Arthur would be telling Akilah or one of their friends another incredible tale about the genius that was Jonathan Patient. If Akilah would question something he said or did, or ask a more intimate question about Mr. P, Arthur would take great offense to any query that implied Jonathan was anything but all-seeing, all-knowing, and generally omnipotent. Arthur would tolerate no questioning of the great man.

Now he wondered if he had simply ignored any clues that his hero was a mere mortal. And once more he was reminded of just how smart his wife was in the ways of the world, how she questioned everything and never took anything for granted.

Jonathan wrote down a name, "Clemente Vivanco," and a phone number.

"Tomorrow morning at ten A.M., I want you to call this number," Mr. P said. "When the man answers it, introduce yourself and ask when might be convenient for you to go out for a visit. Plan on a full day or even overnight; this will not be quick."

"But . . ."

"I don't know if my friend will be able to help you with all of the challenges before you, Arthur. But I will promise you that he will try. He already knows quite a bit about you."

"He does?"

"Of course. I have consulted him many times over the years for guidance when you have reached out to me for help. I have never told you things lightly; I have always used my friend as a sounding board."

Arthur thought for a minute. There was one question

he had to ask, something that Jonathan Patient had to tell him.

"Mr. P—Jonathan—if your own mentor is so smart, why didn't he help you when you were in *my* situation?"

Jonathan sighed heavily.

"Because, my friend, until I lost everything and everyone I loved, I didn't realize how much I needed someone else. I didn't meet him until it was too late.

"Don't let it be too late for you, Arthur. Please don't wait. I couldn't bear to see what happened to me happen to you."

7

The Answer Man's Answer Man

n o man is an island, and this included Jonathan Patient. This improbable truth was still difficult for Arthur to grasp even a week later as he drove across Alligator Alley to Florida's west coast. Normally, Arthur listened to music as he drove from point to point, but today he wanted to be alone with his thoughts—which were essentially the same few questions spinning round and round, their answers not even close to being discovered.

What was Mr. P's terrible secret?

What had happened to his wife and children?

What would Mr. P's mysterious mentor have to tell him that Jonathan could not?

What did Akilah really think about this quest for answers?

Would life with her and their children be better upon his return?

Arthur expected Clemente Vivanco to be akin to King Midas, the mythical man who had all the riches in the world. He must be a brilliant, successful business leader, Arthur thought. Who else could have made Mr. P what he is today?

The GPS mapping device in Arthur's car would only get him so far, Mr. P had warned. After that, finding Clemente's home would take patience and careful attention to Jonathan's handwritten directions.

This, too, puzzled Arthur. How could a man of such great means be off the electronic grid? Wasn't everybody findable these days? Hadn't Google mapped the world with satellites from high above and below with its street-view cameras?

As Arthur took a right turn off US 41 in Fort Myers and began driving east down an unmarked, dusty, one-lane limestone road, he set aside his questions and worried about not sliding off the "road" and into a deep ditch on either side of it. The landscape was flat and unremarkable for the first mile, mostly weeds and untended Florida flora.

But in the second mile, the brush gradually grew thicker and higher. It occurred to Arthur that if his car broke down here, he faced a long, long walk out to get help. He stopped the car momentarily and discovered, as he'd suspected, that his iPhone did not have service here. Go back?

Arthur considered it, briefly, but decided to press on. If there were answers to be found back here in the Florida scrub brush, among the snakes and gators and skeeters, he would stick around and discuss them. The rest of his life was waiting to begin.

About fifteen minutes farther down the road, Arthur saw the first sign of civilization since he'd left the highway: a modest, neatly maintained, one-story ranch house. An elderly man, possibly of Hispanic descent, was slowly but fastidiously sweeping the porch.

"Excuse me, sir," Arthur said, rolling down the passenger window as he pulled up to the man's home.

"Yes?"

"Can you tell me how much farther it is down the road to the home of Clemente Vivanco?"

"But this is the end of the road, young man."

"It is?"

"Yes, Arthur, it is."

"You know my name?"

"I am Clemente, Arthur. Of course I know my guest's name." The old man smiled. "Now why don't you park your car and come inside. I'll bet we could both do with a nice cold glass of lemonade."

Arthur nearly said something he'd regret—he had developed a bad habit of doing so when something in a situation startled him and caught him unprepared. It was another of Akilah's many complaints about his behavior these days.

Fortunately, he caught himself from saying aloud what he couldn't help thinking:

You're Mr. P's Mr. P?

Once inside, Arthur found himself in the home of a man who lived comfortably, if modestly. There were black-and-white photographs from another life scattered about, but nothing that screamed of a man's lifetime of accomplishment; there were no awards, no pictures with celebrities, no shrine to his youth.

In other words, nothing that explained Clemente Vivanco's status or his connection to Mr. P.

"Arthur, please sit down wherever you like."

"Thank you, Mr. Vivanco."

"And please call me Clemente, if you like."

"I . . ."

"Yes, Jonathan said you might not feel comfortable doing that. Perhaps you would rather refer to me as 'Mr. V' for the time being?"

Arthur laughed at himself and for the first time since rolling down the car window to ask for directions, felt himself relax a little. There was no pretense to Clemente Vivanco's home or to the man himself.

"That sounds better, Mr. V," he said, trying it out for the first time.

Then he laughed again.

"What is so funny, Arthur?"

"I just realized I now know a Mr. V, which could stand for 'Victory,' and a Mr. P, which could stand for 'Power.' Power often leads to victory."

Now Clemente Vivanco laughed. "Most of the time, young man, but not always! You might have a lot of power, but if you misuse it or if you eat all your marshmallows, you end up with nothing. Power *with* people, not power *over* people. Big difference, Arthur. Anyway, let's get down to business.

"I realize you have many questions for me, Arthur, and I will do my best to answer them. First, I must warn you that today and tomorrow will be only our introduction. I have a lot to tell you and, after tomorrow, you will have to decide whether it is worth the time of a busy, successful young man such as yourself to return to talk again."

"I . . ."

"No answer necessary now. Let's get started and see where the day takes us, okay?"

Arthur nodded.

"First, you're probably wondering how a jet-setting multimillionaire like Jonathan Patient knows a simple man like me . . .

"When I first met Jonathan, he wasn't the Jonathan you know now. In fact, 'Jonathan Patient' wasn't even his name!"

Arthur's eyes registered his shock. He began to wonder how he could know so little about the man to whom he had entrusted his life and career so many years ago. He said nothing to Clemente Vivanco, leaned forward in his seat, and cushioned himself for more shocks.

"Back then, his name was Barton Shepherd. He was a smart, hardworking man with a beautiful wife and two young children. Barton was the kind of man who was committed to his career, pouring all of his energies into making money but not really understanding why he never made any real progress on his goal of being a rich man.

"He worked long hours, often to the exclusion of his

wife and kids. He loved them—at least he told himself he did—but he never demonstrated that love by making them priorities in his life. His own father had abruptly left his mother when he was very young, so he had no role model for how a good husband and father interacted in family life.

"When he was a young man, just out of college, he somehow believed that acquiring a wife and having children were nothing more than requisite steps on the ladder of success. He didn't realize that a family required more than just a figurehead, and that merely possessing a beautiful spouse and kids didn't make it work; he needed to show up and invest in them much as he would any new business venture.

"Tensions built within the marriage of Barton and his wife. After a whirlwind courtship and the quick arrival of the children, she never imagined a life as lonely as hers became. Barton was never around to participate in the day-to-day and support her. And yet he grew jealous if she ever spent time with anyone outside of himself and the kids. She felt locked in.

"Making the situation even more challenging was that as hard as Barton worked—and as many long hours as he put in—the family was constantly behind on the bills. He spent a lot of money trying to look the part of a successful businessman—the best clothes, a luxury car, eating at the most high-profile restaurants—never considering that if you spent more than you took in, you'd always wind up poorer at the end of the week than when it started.

"Barton's wife might have better tolerated his absences if there weren't a growing stack of bills arriving daily and the collection agencies hadn't started harassing her for payment.

"One day, Barton's wife simply snapped. She had had enough of a husband who was always missing in action and decided to take the kids and move out. After he left for work that morning, she packed the kids, their toys, her clothes, and whatever else her car could carry and headed north on US 41. She left Barton a simple note: 'I can't do this any longer.' As best anyone could tell, she was headed to her parents' home in a tiny northwest Florida fishing village called Cedar Key.

"Somewhere up around Weeki Wachee Springs—that's the tourist trap that boasts of its real-life mermaids—she pulled over for lunch and a bathroom break for the kids.

"That's where something went terribly wrong.

"Leaving the restaurant, she reentered traffic on US 19 and resumed heading north. She wasn't on the road very long when she heard police sirens and then saw flashers heading south. Before she had time to pull off the highway, a stolen car driven by two fleeing young men changed lanes in an effort to evade police. The car crossed over the low, grassy divide between the north- and southbound lanes and was hurtling head-on toward Barton's wife and children. Neither driver had time to swerve and the crash was fiery and total.

"The police arrived just moments later, but it was too late; Barton's family was dead, as were the young men whose car barreled into them at more than one hundred miles an hour."

Arthur realized he needed to breathe. He had no idea how long it had been since he last inhaled.

"All of this was over before Barton knew that his wife had even left him," Mr. V continued. "He was on the road and this was long before anyone carried cell phones. Because the family had few if any friends, no one knew she had left Barton before the police searched their empty home and found her note. And they had no idea where Barton was or how to get in touch with him.

"Barton first learned what happened on the television in a bar he stopped at two days later. He happened to glance up when he heard the evening newscaster mention 'Cedar Key, Florida,' and recognized his wife's car in the video footage. He scrambled to find a local newspaper, which is how he learned the rest of the story."

Arthur felt a tear forming in his left eye. He did nothing

to contain it, instead imagining himself in Mr. P's position. He couldn't imagine the horror of discovering the woman he loved and the beautiful children they produced being horrifically killed—not to mention the trauma that led up to that day.

His first thought was to jump in his car and go right home, to profess his love to his family and rededicate himself to their welfare.

But he didn't get up.

He realized that he was in this stranger's home because Mr. P wanted to prevent a catastrophe of a similar kind from overtaking Arthur's life and splintering his young family. A generation apart, Mr. P had recognized something in Arthur's life that so reminded him of his own mistakes that he decided to expose a part of his past that Arthur could never have dreamed of.

Arthur stayed put. And he was ready with questions.

"Mr. V, that is a horrible, terrifying story. I can barely connect it with the man I know. In fact, I'm hoping you're now going to explain how Barton Shepherd became Jonathan Patient and where you fit into this story."

"Of course, Arthur," Mr. V said. "Let's start with the last part of your question, first.

"I was the owner of the bar that Barton visited that evening. It was a quiet night and I could tell something was truly troubling him when he asked me for the day's newspaper. As he read about the accident, all the energy, all the bravado and salesmanship left Barton Shepherd's being. I didn't know him before that moment, but I would have to say that he was the loneliest-looking man I'd ever seen. And as a man in the business of pouring alcohol, I've seen a lot of lost souls.

"Barton didn't have the energy to get off his stool. He hadn't been drinking much—I think he came into my place mostly to be around people, not to get drunk. He drank black coffee the rest of the night and I sent someone out for a sandwich for him, although he barely had a bite or two.

"By the time closing came around, I knew all about Barton Shepherd. He told me how he'd dedicated his life to work and becoming a big-shot businessman to the exclusion of all else. The guilt he felt at having literally ignored and driven his wife away weighed on him in ways I couldn't begin to imagine.

"I don't think Barton remembered where he was at that point and he didn't seem to have anywhere to go or stay the night. I told him to get in my car and he could stay on my couch—he spent the night right where you're sitting— and that I'd help him sort out the details and get in touch with the authorities in the morning.

"The next day, I made breakfast and Barton thanked

me for taking him in. He asked me a few questions about myself and I told him that I was a Cuban emigrant from the 1960s, that I escaped Fidel Castro's oppression by boat, and restarted my life in Florida with nothing but the shirt on my back and a few hundred dollars. I ran a small night-club in Havana and married—and divorced—young; fortunately, we didn't have any children. My mother had died in a hurricane several years earlier; my father wouldn't leave Cuba even though he hated the authoritarian government. I was an only child and had nothing holding me to the island and decided to find my fortune in America as so many of my brothers in arms before me had done.

"After breakfast, I took Barton back to his car, offered some suggestions to him and we shook hands. He thanked me for whatever kindness I offered and drove off.

"I honestly never expected to see him again."

Mr. V stood and went into his kitchen, leaving Arthur to think about what he had learned so far. His mind was reeling and there was still so much he didn't know or understand.

When Mr. V returned, he was carrying a tray of *ropa vieja* with white rice, black beans, and some delicious-looking plantains. It smelled so good—Arthur hadn't realized how hungry he was. He gratefully accepted the food and it was the best *ropa vieja* he'd ever tasted. Akilah should get the old man's recipe, he thought. Hers was good, but this . . . this was *magnificent.*

"This is delicious, Mr. V. Family recipe?"

"I wish it was! Jonathan said *ropa vieja* was a favorite of yours so I picked some up in town last night. The microwave is a marvelous invention."

Arthur laughed.

"I never did hear from Barton Shepherd again, Arthur."

"No?"

"No. A year passed and I received a letter from Miami. The name on the return address was 'Jonathan Patient,' a name I didn't recognize. Inside was a check for one thousand dollars and a note that read 'Thank you.' It was signed 'JP.'

"I could have used the money, but I didn't know who it was from or why he had sent it. I put the check in my wallet and forgot about it.

"A few months went by and a familiar face turned up at my bar.

" 'Barton!' I said. 'How are you?'

" 'Fine, Clemente, fine,' the man said. 'But it's not Barton anymore. Barton is dead.'

" 'Dead? But you're right here in front of me! What do you mean, dead?'

" 'Barton Shepherd died on the highway with my family,'

he said. 'The man I was no longer served a purpose. His priorities were all wrong, his decisions made for all the wrong reasons, and his life lacked purpose. Not long after I buried my wife and children, I quit my job, moved to Miami, and legally changed my name.'

" 'And who might you be now, my friend?' I asked.

" 'You really haven't guessed?'

" 'No idea.'

" 'I guess not, seeing as how you never cashed the thousand-dollar check.'

"I touched the back pocket where I kept my wallet. 'You're Jonathan Patient? I couldn't figure out why anyone I didn't know would send me a thousand bucks, let alone someone with as ridiculous a name as "Patient." ' That made him laugh.

" 'I turned my life around after that night you took me in,' he said. 'I wanted to do something for you to express my appreciation. Not everyone would have helped a stranger the way you did.'

" 'I beg to differ,' I said. 'Either way, the thank-you note would have sufficed.'

" 'I thought you might say that. Anyway, will you cash the check now?'

" 'Thank you, but no, I don't think so. I don't believe a man should accept payment for doing right by his fellow man who is suffering under the worst possible circumstances. But I appreciate the thought.'

"'Again, I thought you might say that, so I have another idea . . .'"

Jonathan Patient explained to his friend that he was starting a new business and that he needed someone with a different type of mind than his own to call upon for occasional advice and guidance. He didn't want to fall back on his old ways. One of the things that Jonathan was previously guilty of was listening to no one's counsel but his own. The night that fate sent him to Clemente Vivanco's bar, he realized he needed other voices in his life.

"Jonathan made me a minor partner in his new company. It had no assets, no staff, and no sales at that point, but he had a clear vision of what he wanted to accomplish and the kind of entrepreneur he wanted to be.

"More important, he wanted to do for other young men what he felt I had done for him. He wanted me to help him achieve these goals, in exchange for a portion of any future profits. I don't know much about running any other business than a bar and I had no idea where his life might take him, so I accepted his invitation. I figured it would never amount to anything and I didn't want to accept his thousand-dollar check.

"Little did I understand that day how driven the newly

born Jonathan Patient truly was. He was determined to right the perceived wrongs in his previous life. And while he knew it would never bring back his wife and children, he prayed that somehow, somewhere, they knew he was trying. Not a day went by that he wasn't driven by their memory and his loss."

It dawned on Arthur that—based on how wealthy he knew Jonathan to be—Clemente Vivanco must be an incredibly rich man, despite his humble surroundings. For the first time since he arrived, Arthur wondered what time it was. He looked outside and discovered the sun had long since set.

A yawn escaped his mouth before he realized it was happening. Embarrassment registered on his face but Clemente took no offense.

"What an inconsiderate host I am; you had a long day getting here and then you had to listen to an old man yammering for hours. Where are my manners? Let's get you some bedding and you can make yourself comfortable on the couch. At least I'm assuming you're still planning to stay the night?"

"Yes, thank you, Mr. V. I'm way too tired to drive home tonight."

"Good, good! And tomorrow, we'll turn our attention to your own situation."

No Man Is a Marshmallow Island

In the years that followed Clemente Vivanco's first introduction to Jonathan Patient, the older man discovered that he had developed a philosophy of life that wasn't apparent until Jonathan himself identified it.

Mr. V recognized that its roots were not, in fact, with him but with his father. Which was somewhat ironic, in that when he was in his late teens he reached a point where he felt he had to choose between two distinct paths and spheres of influence.

On the one side, there was his father, a man who worked hard from sunup till sundown but always had time for family. He never had an unkind word for anyone and treated everyone he met, friend and stranger alike, with kindness and respect.

And on the other side was the infamous Dominican ambassador in Cuba and ultimate playboy, Porfirio Rubirosa. Rubirosa—who was a dear friend of his father's despite the wide difference in their personalities and makeup—was a womanizer of the first kind, a gambler and a heavy drinker. He took chances—very often risks—every day and lived a life that was bigger and more colorful than anyone else's in all of pre-revolutionary Cuba.

Clemente considered his father's quiet, steady life and compared it against Rubirosa's loud style, the ever-present company of the island's most beautiful women, the daily political intrigue and rumormongering. For a young man in the heady, pre-Castro days, there was no choice really. Clemente Vivanco chose to follow Rubirosa and live every day like it was his last.

Totally different values, utterly different principles.

That was the choice he made. And it was fun—for a few years. But the lifestyle—and the resentment it created among his friends and family—ironically pushed Clemente to go in a different direction at roughly the same time he bid a heavy farewell to his father and fled Fidel Castro's Cuba for the United States.

But he still wanted to go his own way, leaving behind family and friends. Unlike most Cubans, Clemente went not to Miami, the final destination of so many emigrants of the era, but to Southwest Florida and Fort Myers, where he could reshape his persona out of sight of people who knew him the way he once was.

As owner of a series of progressively bigger and better bars and later, nightclubs, Clemente made a fair living using the nightclub skills he learned at the bent elbow of Porfirio Rubirosa—but tempered his personal lifestyle by at last emulating his father's best characteristics of respect, restraint, and thrift.

Over time, Clemente allowed people from his old life to know the man he had become and welcomed them back into his current existence. To a one they were surprised by the way he had altered his life's trajectory through sheer force of will and determination. The people who were once his friends wanted to be his friends again. And he found creative ways to support his father—who never left Cuba— and took pride in demonstrating that he had become his father's true son after all.

•   •   •

Over breakfast, Clemente Vivanco told Arthur about his own evolution and how he now made his personal choices and went about his business according to sixteen essential principles. They were:

1. The *implementation* of knowledge is power.

2. Your life is your own damn fault.

3. Know who you are.

4. Develop self-discipline.

5. Go to the edge.

6. Help others get what *they* want.

7. People do what they do for a reason.

8. Always be honest with yourself.

9. Close your mouth and open your ears.

10. Live your life one day at a time.

11. Be tender with the young and compassionate with the old.

12. Example is the most effective way to influence others.

13. Greatness comes from the recognition that your potential is limited by the degree of your commitment and persistence.

14. Continuous improvement must be a way of life.

15. **Stop procrastinating.**

16. **Accept responsibility, look within, act.**

As their second day together wore on and Arthur prepared to drive home, Mr. V asked Arthur if he had enough.

"What do you mean by 'enough'?" Arthur asked. "Are you saying there is more?"

Mr. V laughed.

"Arthur, did you think you would gain as much knowledge as Jonathan possesses today in one overnight trip? Like going to Boy Scout camp to learn how to start a fire with nothing but dry leaves and branches?"

"No, no, of course not. I just thought . . ."

As it turned out, the list of sixteen principles just scratched the surface of what Clemente Vivanco proposed to share with Arthur. An appetizer, if you will, ahead of the full menu.

Mr. V said the laws were just empty platitudes without some understanding of what each means and how to apply it to life's daily challenges.

On Jonathan Patient's advice, he offered to explain one law a week to Arthur.

"Every week for the next sixteen weeks, I will teach you one of my laws, which will give you time to absorb and apply it," Mr. V said. "Each time you return to me, I will introduce you to the next. In four months' time, you will know a lot of what Jonathan and I know."

Arthur's first reaction was horror—he couldn't wait four months! His world was unraveling *now*!

Clemente saw this in Arthur's eyes and smiled pleasantly.

"I know what you're thinking: 'Why can't the old man just explain all of his laws to me now? Why drag this out? Is this just a lonely old man ensuring he'll have a visitor in his old age?' "

Now it was Arthur's turn to relax and laugh.

"You're right on the first two," he admitted. "But the third never crossed my mind. Honest!"

Mr. V put his hand on Arthur's shoulder in a paternal manner that Arthur found reassuring.

"I once heard an immensely successful American businessman say that he read somewhere that people only remember ten percent of what they hear and read. So he made it a point of repeating things ten times, figuring it improved the odds that his employees would remember what *he* said.

"I don't know if that worked," Mr. V said, "but the point of it made an impression on me: You can't overload people with information, no matter how well intended it may be. I know you could go on the Internet with your smartphone and have the information riches of the world in your hand anytime you wish. But having it and absorbing and applying it are different things. If you want to know what I know, you'll have to do it my way."

"I understand," Arthur said. "I'm in."

"Great," Clemente said. "See you next week."

The Reeducation of Arthur: Part One

For the next sixteen weeks, Arthur sat in Clemente Vi-vanco's living room, determined to master all that the old man could teach him. He made a commitment to himself—and his family and business—to see the process through to the end. He had bought a special journal in which he took careful notes, knowing that the words he was transcribing—Mr. V's words—would form a literal manual for success.

Week 1

The *implementation* of knowledge is power. Francis Bacon said, "Knowledge is power." That's true, but he should have said something else. He should have said, "Applied knowledge is power." If you *know* and you don't *do*, you don't know.

In reality, no one cares what you know. No one cares how many titles you hold. What people care about are results. In other words what you *do* with what you *know*.

It is so easy to say, "Apply what you know," "Implement your plans," and "Do what you know how to do," yet it is terribly difficult to do so.

Most people know what has to be done, yet they don't do it. Most people know that they should exercise at least five days a week and keep a healthy diet. They know what exercises they should do, they have a good idea of how many calories each food contains but where they fail is in the execution of this knowledge.

So, implement and you win. Know and do nothing—you lose.

Week 2

Your life is your own damn fault. Assume full responsibility for it. Learn what you need to do to fix it or at least change your circumstances. Take action as soon as you feel you have learned what you need to know, but don't be paralyzed by trying to do it perfectly. Perfect is the enemy of good unless you are flying a plane with 250 passengers aboard. In that setting, you must be perfect or the plane might crash.

Don't blame everything that happens to you on other people. Wherever you are, whatever you decided, whatever you've chosen—that's who you are. Everything you decide affects what happens next. You are the sum of everything you think and everything you do and no one else can be responsible for it.

People tend to blame everything around them for their not being successful or not reaching their goals. But everyone must understand the bottom line: We're each responsible for our own results and our own failures. What we do and how we perform is all based on the way we think. Even though you may have been dealt a bad hand by the universe or by nature or by God or whatever you believe in—some people say this is luck—in the final analysis, it's how you handle those cards that matters. If you go to a blackjack table and you're dealt a sixteen and the bank has a ten, the dealer has one card yet to be revealed. Your chances of succeeding are extremely low. However, you can either stay or you can ask for a card. At least you have some options and with a little luck you may win.

There will be moments in life when you really have no options, points at which you are not even in the game. The guy who has a sixteen while the bank has a ten and a hidden card could still win if he draws a five and the bank has another ten. The guy standing behind him, not playing but wanting to play? He *definitely* can't win. There might be situations in life where you want to be in the game but the game doesn't want you. You are out and you want in. Even so, you have choices. For example, you can invent a new game altogether, set the rules, and find some new people to play it. You can buy the position that someone has in the table so that you can sit and play. You may form a partnership with someone sitting at the table if you can offer some value to them so that he or she considers your offer.

No matter how bleak things look, all of us have options in life—that's the meaning of this law.

Week 3

Know who you are. Know where you are now in life. Take responsibility for who you are and where you are now in life.

Know damn well what your strengths and weaknesses are. Most people make the mistake of concentrating on their weaknesses and trying to fix them. That takes a lot of work and very often you will never be able to overcome those weaknesses.

On the other hand, when you identify your strengths, you can build on them. Your strengths are your talents and your talents are your gifts. Use them to your advantage.

You must be realistic and accept where you are in life right now. Why is it that you have not been promoted? Why are you stuck? Why do you feel you have no future?

Discovering the answer to these questions will solve the question of where you are now in life. Then comes another important question: What do I have to change in order to further my position in life? What skills must I acquire? Am I willing to sacrifice my time and my money in order to acquire those skills? Do I really want to make the investment? Most people stop right here. They ask those questions and their answer is that it is too much trouble, they have no time, they can't get the money, or find the time to do what needs to be done. Because there are so many people who think that way, those who think differently are the ones who, in the end, will win. You must realize that lots of jobs are disappearing because of technology, and you must notice the manner in which the world is subsequently changing. If you are not willing to acquire new skills, to retrain yourself and look at what careers are more promising, at which industries will advance, you are in for a rough ride in the coming economy.

Week 4

Develop self-discipline. Don't eat all your marshmallows. Don't allow the need for immediate gratification to take you down the wrong path.

Developing self-discipline is not an easy thing, but first, let's define it.

Self-discipline describes your ability to control and motivate yourself, to stay on track and do what you perceive you need to do in order to achieve an objective or a goal you have in mind.

"Don't eat all your marshmallows" can have different meanings.

Let's look at it from a financial point of view. If you *make* $500 a week and you *spend* $500 a week, that's you eating all of your marshmallows. If you make $500 a week and you spend $600 a week, you are not only eating all your marshmallows, you are heading straight to bankruptcy. This law applies to citizens, to companies, to communities, and to countries. In fact, that is what is happening to most countries in the world, including us, unfortunately.

This need for instant gratification is what is taking us down the wrong path.

Let's apply this to sales. Let's say that you are selling a product and a client says to you, "I want product A," and you say, "Great, I have it, when do you want it delivered?" What happened? You *ate* the marshmallows. If you instead told the client, "Mr. X, we have product A and it is indeed an excellent product, but let me ask you, what problems are you having that you think product A will solve?" When the client answers that question and you ask other good questions, you might be able to walk out of there with a much bigger sale, maybe products A, B, C, and D.

Jonathan Patient once visited a client who wanted to hire him to do a time management seminar for his company. Jonathan does time management seminars but if he had said, "Sure, how many people, what day, and where are we going to do it?" he would have eaten the marshmallow.

Instead, he said, "Mr. Client, I do a fine time management seminar, but let me ask you, what is happening in your company that you think a time management seminar will solve?" The answer to that question led Jonathan to other questions and he finally secured an order for seminars totaling $1.2 million instead of $10,000. *That* is the power of understanding the marshmallow principle.

Week 5

Go to the edge. Get out of your comfort zone. Do things that others are not willing to do. Remember that successful people are willing to do things that unsuccessful people are not willing to do. Welcome failure. Yes, welcome failure. But fail early and fail forward. A failure is a lesson learned, and if you are not failing you are not risking and you are not growing. If you are not growing, you are dying.

If you do not fail, or if you're not failing enough, you're not getting out of your comfort zone.

The proof that you are out of your comfort zone is that you are attempting things that will not work or will even fail because you are in new territory. Your comfort zone is what you know. Your comfort zone is what you're familiar with.

Don't fail in a big way, or in a way that will take you down. Fail a little. Fail early. Fail forward. Fail in a way that if you try something new, and it does not work, you live to succeed or fail another day.

James Cameron, the director of two of the most successful movies in motion picture history, *Avatar* and *Titanic*, has a four-point formula for success:

1. **Curiosity** is "the most powerful thing you own."
2. **Imagination** is "a force that can actually manifest a reality."
3. **Respect** is "more important than all the laurels in the world."
4. **Failure** is an option; Cameron says you need to take risks and that taking risks always runs the risk of failure.

At NASA, there is a famous sign that says, "Failure is not an option."

Cameron disagrees.

He believes that failure is always an option because otherwise you would never risk anything. You would never leave your comfort zone.

Week 6

Help others get what *they* want. Then they will help you get what *you* want. This is teamwork. No one can do it by themselves. You need other people to work with you and help you reach your goals. But it is important that those who help you also win. Win-win is always important.

As part of Jonathan Patient's company's policy, whenever a client hires him to speak to a company or professional association, he does something that others are not willing to do. He says, "Mr. Client, I am so grateful that you hired me to do this particular job. And I want to go an extra step as part of my gratitude. I am offering to make a second speech to someone you think needs it in your community. It could be four people. It could be a school. It could be a hospital. It could be a sports team—anyone you think would be helped by my presentation." The client builds tremendous goodwill, and Jonathan wins because he reaches people who would have never, ever been able to hear his message, so everything is a win-win. That is an example of doing something that others are not willing to do and that helps others get what they want.

Week 7

People do what they do for a reason. In other words, it is important to identify the causes of your behavior and that of others.

When we look at ourselves, we don't always see our self-interest. In reality, everyone acts according to his or her own self-interest. If you have empathy—if you put yourself in another person's shoes—you're better able to identify why it is that they act the way do. And then you understand them. In *The 7 Habits of Highly Effective People*, Stephen R. Covey wrote, "Seek first to understand, then to be understood." Do this and you will have a better chance of understanding the other person, seeing why they act the way they do. Realize that in life, everyone acts according to his or her own self-interest.

Week 8

Always be honest with yourself. The harm done by living in denial is enormous. Look in the mirror and ask yourself, "Am I being honest?"

Be realistic in regards to what you're good at and what you're not good at. You should appraise your strengths and your weaknesses so you can accentuate your strengths.

You have to be honest and then work with whatever you have to your greatest advantage. If you concentrate on fixing your weaknesses, you may never accomplish your goals.

In his mind, Arthur thought he took responsibility for his life, but the more he reflected on it, the more he recognized that he tended to blame others when things didn't go according to plan for him. Sure, sometimes other people did interfere with his best-laid plans. But often he looked for someone or something to blame, some excuse, such as blaming a bad day at the office on a fight with Akilah the night before or on her withholding physical intimacy, which often left him frustrated and unable to sleep.

Now, he realized he had a hand in those disagreements and even in her withholding physical intimacy. For instance, he could have done things that would have better laid a path for intimacy, but often he wanted to skip past them to get to satisfaction. He knew, after years of marriage, that Akilah was not going to have relations with him after eleven P.M. It created havoc with her schedule the next day, and she was nothing if not devoted to her schedule, thanks to child-care concerns and running the restaurant. Arthur, on the other hand, did what he wanted, when he wanted, with little regard for the clock or how his needs disrupted the lives of the people around him.

Those were big issues that he recognized and worked hard at improving. He could tell progress was being made because Akilah had been more receptive to him in the last eight weeks—sometimes even initiating activity at night when he was particularly attentive to her needs during the day.

Just subjecting himself to learning the principles for four months of informal study was definitely taking Arthur out of his comfort zone. But Jonathan Patient believed it was necessary, so he was going to stick with it—even if he could really use the same time and energy to make more money and expand his client base.

Over the weeks, he realized that meeting with Clemente Vivanco was not unlike the one week a month he had come in off the road to chauffeur Charlie Slow around and learn about running a business. That had turned out pretty well, right?

Arthur smiled. What could possibly be bad about sitting at the feet of an elderly Cuban man and absorbing his lifetime of knowledge? *It worked out for Mr. P—why not me, too?*

Akilah didn't ask her husband many questions about his trips to Fort Myers. It was enough for her that Jonathan Patient had taken a hand in her husband's personal well-being after so many years of guiding his career and business relationships. She was content to give Arthur some time to sort things out.

Some time, she thought. *I won't wait forever.*

In his first days back home, Akilah sensed Arthur was just as lost in thought as before he had met Clemente Vivanco. But something was different as the weeks went on. He asked a lot more questions about what was going on in her life, how her day was, what she was thinking about. And the interest was *sincere*. That was different than before. Arthur still forgot things, but they weren't as important as not remembering to pick up the kids after school. In fact, he seemed highly attuned to the whereabouts of his wife and the twins.

Another difference: When Arthur did forget something, he was apoplectic with guilt and apologized profusely. He promised to work harder to get things right.

What was especially different was that he chose not to share any details of his conversations with Mr. V with her. That was odd, because whenever he returned home from a lunch or visit with Jonathan Patient, Arthur couldn't wait to share what he learned, knowing Akilah might benefit as much or more than he would.

But Akilah didn't mind this silence because Arthur was changing so much. Day by day, Akilah lowered her defenses ever so slightly. She was friendlier to Arthur than she had been before he met Clemente Vivanco and he returned her kindnesses twofold.

Akilah also noticed that he was making fewer between-meals trips to the refrigerator for snacks and that his weight—long on the rise—seemed to be coming down. His face was less puffy and his color was better.

Something was definitely different. In a good way.

10

The Reeducation of Arthur: Part Two

Knowing where he was going and what he would find at the end of the deserted limestone road made the drive back to Clemente Vivanco's home go by much more quickly as he arrived to start the second half of his lessons.

The only thing that was different this time was the letter Arthur received advising him to "bring comfortable old shoes and clothes."

Maybe the air-conditioning in the old house wasn't working?

When Arthur pulled up to the house, the sun was setting and Mr. V was right where Arthur had seen him the first time, sweeping the porch. He waved to Arthur and walked over to the car to greet him with a handshake and a hug.

"Welcome back, Arthur!" Clemente said. "I hope you had a pleasant ride over from Miami."

"Very nice, very peaceful, Mr. V. A lot of time to be alone with my thoughts and get my head right for the next two days," Arthur said.

"Wonderful, wonderful," Mr. V said. "I certainly hope you came prepared to get right to work!"

Mr. V took Arthur's overnight bag and brought it into the living room, setting it on the couch where Arthur knew he would spend the next night.

"Absolutely, sir. What will we be talking about first?"

"No talk right now," Mr. V said. "First I need you to do some chores for me."

"Chores?"

"Nothing too strenuous, just some things around the house and garden that need doing," Mr. V said, walking through the living room into the tidy kitchen and out the back door as Arthur followed, mystified.

"I didn't know I'd be doing chores for you, Mr. V. *Um . . .* why *am* I doing chores?"

"Arthur, too many people in this world believe that the things they get in life are only worth what they paid for them. Jonathan told me that as you've become more successful in life, you've developed a taste for luxury items. Nothing wrong with that, of course; you earn good money so you're entitled to spend more money to get things you perceive as having a higher value, right?"

"Riiiiiight . . ."

"But Jonathan and I are concerned that if I simply give you all of the information in my possession that you won't value it as much as if it cost you something."

"I see," Arthur said. "But couldn't I just pay you for your time?"

"I don't want or need your money, Arthur. But there are quite a few things that need doing around my home, things that Jonathan no longer has the youth and vigor to keep up with."

"Wait. *Wait!* You're saying that Mr. P has been doing maintenance and chores around your house all these years?" Arthur was stunned. Again and again he discovered just how little he knew about his longtime mentor.

"How do you think he maintains that healthy complexion and muscle tone of his? Fancy gyms and tanning salons?" Mr. V laughed. "Jonathan has been coming out to the ranch every three months like clockwork for the last two decades."

"I never dreamed you could have that much to teach me, Mr. V," Arthur said.

"Oh, Arthur!" Clemente laughed. "Jonathan was largely done learning from me after four months, same as you will be. He kept coming back because he liked doing it. He could drop out of sight for a few days here or a week there, be reminded why he made so many changes in his life, and get a productive workout, too.

"And, of course, I fed him well. I know *all* the best places for takeout in Fort Myers."

Arthur set out to do the chores Mr. V directed him to, and later that night, enjoying the feel of an honest day's work in his oft-unused muscles, he took out his journal and carefully took notes on the next lessons Mr. V shared.

Week 9

Listen more. You learn little by talking all the time. **Close your mouth and open your ears.**

God gave us two ears and one mouth for a reason: so we can listen twice as much as we talk.

Most people don't want to listen that much and they want to talk *a lot*. Why? Because they want to make themselves understood instead of trying to understand. Understand others, and then be understood yourself—that means listen to the other person.

Week 10

Live your life one day at a time. Do it and you will eliminate 80 percent of your worries about yesterday and tomorrow. Treasure every moment that you have. Just like the old saying that the past is a canceled check, the future is a promissory note, but the present is money in the bank.[2] Every day, identify one good thing about your life and concentrate on that.

People worry quite a bit. They worry over stuff that's already happened—about that which they can no longer do anything. Accept the facts as facts. Deal with what's real. Nothing will change what's done; live in the present. Examine how you deal with the negative in your life. Don't worry about things you cannot control.

A lot of people worry about the future. Don't be one of them. Concentrate on what you can do that may influence today, the events that lie ahead. Focus on whatever you can do to better your circumstances. Do that and you'll be much happier and more productive.

One technique is to look at something good in your life

---

[2] This quote has been attributed to several different people, including George Bernard Shaw, Hubert Tinley, and Kay Lyons: http://thinkexist.com/quotation/yesterday_is_a_canceled_check-tomorrow_is_a/168532.html.

every day. For example, if you get up in the morning and see it's a sunny day, remember, *You're not blind! You can see!* Can you imagine the number of people who are sightless, who cannot ever appreciate the brightness of the sun and the beauty its light creates everywhere? So if you look at today that way, you're pretty lucky. Maybe you're going outside to jog a bit. Do you know how many people in wheelchairs would kill to do that?

Concentrate on all the good things that you have going for you and expound on them instead of thinking about scenarios in the future that might never come to pass. Don't fortune-tell. Live in the present!

Week 11

Be tender with the young and compassionate with the old. Encourage those who strive and be tolerant with the weak, the wrong, and the uninformed. Over the course of your life you will have been all of them. Make it a habit to do a good deed every single day.

This is a law that suggests you should be a good person all the time—not just when it suits or benefits you. Sometimes you're driving and you see an elderly person driving slowly.

Don't honk your horn at him. Don't cuss at him. Don't scream at him because one day you'll be old and you'll be driving that same car on that same busy road and you will not want somebody else doing that to *you*.

Sometimes you might encounter someone who is wrong. Wrong about *this* or *that*. What makes them wrong? Understand where they come from. Try to understand their point of view. Consider how they were raised. Understand that they were taught differently than you and might be the way they are because they grew up under circumstances that made them that way. Demonstrate tolerance for people who are different than you. Perhaps they made a few wrong choices along the way. Instead of verbally accosting them, try to educate them so they can be better. And with the weak, there will be times when you will be in situations where *you* are the weak one. None of us is always on top of our game. There will be times when you can't draw on all your strength. You're going to be in situations where *you* are that person who, at that moment, is in a weak negotiating position. Understand that if you are dealing with someone in a weak situation, you shouldn't step on their throats with the heel of your shoe. Don't push them down. On the contrary, try to help them out because they are weak. That will one day come back to you when you need it.

Week 12

Example is the most effective way to influence others. Walk your talk. Keep your promises. Be on time. Pay your bills.

You cannot lecture people when you yourself are not doing what you are talking about. Walk the walk; talk the talk. The most effective way to influence people is for you to set the example. You have to be fair. You have to give everyone a chance. Treat people with respect! Some executives and middle managers scream at people and insult them. It doesn't matter what they say. It doesn't carry any weight. The only way that people will accept what you're saying and respect, understand, and follow you is if you lead by example. They must see in your behavior what you are talking about. Otherwise, your words have no value.

People *will* criticize you. People *will* do things to derail and stop you. People might put obstacles in your way. But in the end, it all comes down to you, to your attitude, to the way you think. Either you allow them to win and you're out of the game, or you just decide that no one can or will stop you. Simply decide you will look for another way. Be creative. Reinvent yourself. Seek help. Do things that will allow you to climb over the obstacles that have been placed in your path by others.

Over four months, Arthur learned to drive a farm tractor, washed Clemente's classic 1992 Cadillac convertible several times, took his mentor to a series of doctors' appointments, and generally accommodated the older man's every request. He never said no to Mr. V, never implied that a task was beneath him nor impugned the man's motives.

And whatever he did, wherever they went, Clemente kept talking, sharing stories, making observations about people and places that Arthur would have previously never noticed.

When there was a task he would have preferred not to do, Arthur thought of the ways in which a parent often did things for young children that they could not yet do for themselves. And he found himself thinking about the twins and how he never took pleasure in the mundane, day-to-day events in their lives, and he asked himself, "Why not?" If he could do these things for an old man he hardly knew, why not do the things his own flesh and blood needed from him? Why should Akilah have to do it all? It hadn't escaped his notice over the years that she seemed to actually enjoy doing these things; why, he had never grasped.

He chuckled to himself as he realized there was a lesson hidden somewhere in his own realization. He just couldn't identify it yet.

"Not losing your concentration already, are you, Arthur?" Mr. V asked.

"Not at all, sir. Just thinking about my kids, that's all. How they would enjoy seeing their dad harvesting oranges from trees—or even doing it themselves!"

"Maybe you could bring them along sometime," Mr. V said.

"Really, sir? I think they'd enjoy that."

"Why not? Take some of the mystery out of what you're doing here. Maybe the three of you could make an adventure of it—and, at the same time, give your wife a day or two off."

"I . . . I don't think I've ever been alone with the kids for more than a few hours at a time," Arthur said, somewhat embarrassed by the realization. "But I'm always leaving Akilah alone with the kids for days at a time when I travel on business. It never occurred to me that that was an imposition or that maybe she'd like to get away from the three of us sometimes."

"Maybe she would, maybe she wouldn't," Mr. V said. "Maybe she'd just like the option."

"I wonder why I never saw that on my own?" Arthur said.

"Nothing like a little fresh air and a man getting his hands dirty and his back out of joint thanks to heavy lifting to get the mind in gear," Mr. V said. "Now you keep on working and we'll move on."

Week 13

Some people are more intelligent than others. Some are more talented than others. Some are more educated than others, but we all have the capacity to be great. **Greatness comes from the recognition that your potential is limited by the degree of your commitment and persistence.** In other words, by your attitude. So choose your attitude *carefully*.

You may be more or less intelligent than others. You may have more or less talent. You will be more or less educated. Those are factors that might have an influence on how you do, but the one thing that will get you over the hump, the one thing you always have to treasure and develop is having a positive attitude. In other words, thinking that you can always find a way.

Have the self-discipline to not allow bad stuff to get ahold of you and misdirect your actions. Make sure that you always keep a positive attitude, even though sometimes you might feel sad. Sometimes things might go wrong. Sometimes you will lose an important game or deal. But even though that happens, you cannot see it as a defeat. You must see it as a valuable lesson that only a loss can gift you. I maintain that people learn from adversity and that is what they sometimes need in order to rise up, little by little, through sometimes crushing defeats, and sustain themselves to eventual victory.

Week 14

If you find a good solution and become too attached to it, the solution may become your next problem. Even if you find a good solution, always look for ways to improve it. **Continuous improvement must be a way of life.**

Success can be your biggest enemy, because it makes some people complacent. You go into a comfort zone. You think that you'll always be successful and so you stop thinking of ways to improve yourself because you're successful *right now.* You stop looking for other ways to grow your success, or you simply bask in your existing success and become negligent about feeding it.

Strangely enough, success is the main enemy of a lot of successful companies. They fail because they fail to act. They fail to change. They fail to analyze why they are successful. Are they successful because they have such a good team, or are they successful because their competitors are inept? Maybe their main competitor made a bad decision. But what happens when that incompetent competitor goes out of business? A new competitor comes into the picture and maybe they're not as inept as the last one. Maybe the successful company isn't that good; maybe they're average and achieved success because their competition was worse. If they want to stay ahead, now they must be smarter!

Don't just analyze failure; make sure you understand why you're successful.

Week 15

If you won't start, it is a safe bet you won't finish. **Stop procrastinating.** Get on with it! The late great speaker Zig Ziglar used to say, "Anything worth doing is worth doing poorly until you can learn to do it well."

You should never fall into analysis paralysis. In other words, make sure you don't want to do something so perfectly that *you never start*! Make sure you don't overanalyze in an effort to prevent all mistakes.

This happens to a lot of would-be writers—people who spend years *talking* about writing a book, but never actually write a word. They want to write the perfect book, but they never even start.

You have to start somewhere. When you start a business, you no doubt want it to be the perfect business. You want all the conditions to be right in order for you to start the business, but that never happens so you procrastinate and never start the business. When someone says, "Someday I will write a book," "Someday I will visit Europe," "Someday I will own my own home," do you know what "someday" means? For most people, someday means never. *Ever.* Put your goals in your calendar and identify what steps need to be taken in order to meet them or your dreams will never happen.

Week 16

When you constantly blame others, you have given up your power to change. **Accept responsibility, look within, act.**

It comes back to the same principle that you are responsible for your own success. If you are constantly blaming circumstances or other people, what does that mean? You lose control, because if you blame somebody else, that means it's out of your hands.

If you're saying you are not successful because of the economy, because of the president of your country, the boss, your employees, your managers, the products, or the awful marketing, you'll never be successful because you have no control over those things. Start assuming responsibility. Say, "You know what? I might have bad marketing. I might have a bad manager. This company might not be the best company in the world, but if I do what I need to do, if I take responsibility, if I look at ways to be more creative, if I find more ways of selling this stuff, ways to go around the obstacles that I'm facing right now, I'll *be* successful." Having that mind-set is totally different than using excuses for everything wrong that happens to you.

Of the second half of the sixteen essential principles, Arthur was especially drawn to #9 ("Close your mouth and open your ears"), #12 ("Example is the most effective way to influence others") and #16 ("Accept responsibility, look within, act").

He recognized that these principles matched up to his current issues especially well. Arthur had long been more entertained and informed by the sound of his own voice over most others, with the exception—usually—of Jonathan Patient's and Charlie Slow's. But now he had been exposed to Mr. V's wisdom, and during this learning process, he had been reminded of Akilah's sure wisdom. If these four people knew so many things that could inform his life so profoundly, there were probably more voices he could learn from in the future if only he shut up and allowed them to reach him.

As a father, it never sank in before that if his actions didn't align with his words, his own children wouldn't be influenced by him the way he had hoped. Akilah called him a hypocrite at times because while he was eating all his marshmallows, he was admonishing his children and clients to not eat theirs! "Walk the walk, talk the talk" wasn't just a fancy line: It was a way of life Arthur needed to adopt both at home and in the office.

And all sixteen of the essential principles could be found under the umbrella of the last one for Arthur: "Accept responsibility, look within, act." In this, he had a lot of work ahead for himself, but recognizing the challenge, he hoped, would be a big step toward overcoming it.

11

Sharing the Marshmallow

onths three and four and the second set of Clemente Vivanco's sixteen essential principles came easier than the first, but there were a few that caused Arthur to stumble. He expected Clemente to chastise him for failing, but Mr. V actually congratulated Arthur for mastering and committing to as many as he could.

Arthur was particularly encouraged because things at home were going more smoothly than ever with Akilah and the kids, who all sensed a big change in him. And Mr. P complimented him as well on embracing change so thoroughly and honoring their now-common mentor by Arthur living his life the way it was meant to be lived.

• • •

As Arthur and Mr. V approached their final evening together, Arthur had a surprise for his patron: Akilah, the twins, and Jonathan Patient drove up the long dusty drive.

It was the first time that Arthur had ever surprised Clemente, and what a delicious surprise it was! As the kids rushed out of the brightly colored Just Ask catering van and up the front porch to hug their father and shake hands with the utterly speechless Mr. V, Akilah and Jonathan went around to the back of the vehicle and started unloading trays of food.

"Mr. V, I think you already know Mr. P!" Arthur said with a laugh. "And this"—he wrapped an arm around Akilah and gave her an affectionate kiss on the cheek—"is the lovely and talented star of my life, Akilah!"

"Akilah, *que belleza de mujer!* It is such a delight to see you in the flesh," Clemente said. "You are every bit as beautiful and radiant as Arthur and Jonathan said you were."

Akilah grinned. "Jonathan said that, too, did he?"

Jonathan just blushed and managed a weak smile.

Everyone laughed.

"Please, please, come in! Come in! I'm afraid my home

is rather humble and I don't get many visitors, but *mi casa es su casa*. And all this food! Is there anything left in your restaurant for the paying customers?"

Inside, Akilah and Arthur took the food to the kitchen and began bringing out appetizer platters of fried plantains, shrimp, salmon, and *jamon serrano y queso*. While they did this, Clemente and Jonathan talked in hushed tones. They were somewhat serious, but smiling.

The children occupied themselves with some old board games Clemente brought out for them, becoming fascinated with the pop-up die container on the Trouble board. That gave the grown-ups time to talk without interruption.

"Mr. V," Arthur said, "you've done so much for me—and for Jonathan—that we all agreed it was time to do something special for you. You wouldn't accept payment from either of us for all you've contributed to our success, so we thought we'd throw a little party for you and fill your refrigerator with a week's worth of homemade meals from Just Ask."

"This *is* a surprise! And I couldn't imagine one that could taste any better," Mr. V said. "Akilah, you are as wonderful a cook as I've been hearing. This food is magnificent!"

"Thank you, Mr. V," Akilah said. "There are a few off-menu items here, such as *rabo encendido* and *cordero*, because Arthur said those were your favorites."

"This is so much better than any of the restaurants around here could ever prepare!"

"I'm glad you like it," Arthur said, "because we're opening a Just Ask Again here in Fort Myers next week. And we'll be bringing you all of your favorites every week—if you don't mind adding us to your restaurant rotation!"

"I am truly speechless," Mr. V said.

Jonathan and Arthur burst into laughter.

"That's a first!" Jonathan said.

"Hear, hear!" Arthur agreed, laughing.

Soon it was time for the entree and everyone came to the table as Arthur and Akilah brought out lobster thermidor, and white rice with potatoes.

As they sat down, Arthur asked for everyone's attention.

"Most men—and women—are lucky to have a single mentor, someone who takes an interest in their lives and careers and lends them the benefit of their experience to help make them better, more successful people. I have been most fortunate to have not one but four such people in my life."

"Four, Arthur?" Akilah asked, perplexed.

"Four, dear," her husband said. "First, of course, there was Jonathan Patient, who saw potential in a mere chauffeur and shared with him the original marshmallow theory.

"That inspired me to stop wasting my time and money in frivolous, unproductive ways. I went to college and landed a great job with SlowDown! Inc., where my second mentor, Charlie Slow, put me back behind the wheel and taught me a whole new range of skills.

"Unfortunately, while Jonathan and Charlie sharpened my business skills, I lost touch with the most important part of my life—husband and father. Jonathan recognized this and introduced me to Clemente Vivanco, who we're celebrating tonight. I think my time with Mr. V has helped bring balance and greater well-being to my life and the way I live it. At least I hope it has."

Mr. V, Mr. P, and Akilah applauded, with the twins joining in just because it was fun.

"Well said, Arthur," Mr. P said.

"Indeed," confirmed Mr. V. "I think it's safe to say this has become a graduation party, Arthur. Well earned, indeed. You've worked hard—both on learning my life laws and around my house. The garden has never been more beautiful! Sorry, Jonathan!"

"No need to apologize, Clemente. I heartily agree," Mr. P said. "I never did get the hang of gardening. But Arthur appears to be quite the natural."

Akilah was quiet during the joking. Arthur could see that something was on her mind.

"What is it, Akilah?" he asked. "What are you thinking about?"

"You said you had four mentors. I only counted three—Jonathan, Charlie, and Clemente. Who was the fourth?"

All three men around the table smiled.

Arthur started to answer, but his precocious son Orly beat him to it.

"I know, Daddy, I know!" he said.

"Okay, Orly. Who is it?"

"That's easy—it's Mommy, right?"

Akilah didn't see that one coming.

"That's correct, my boy. Your mother is number four."

"Me?" Akilah said, confused.

"Who else could it be?" Arthur said, putting his hand warmly on his wife's shoulder. "Think about it: Who challenged me to act like a man when she discovered after college graduation that I was a penniless fraud? Who taught me to recognize love? Who has patiently helped me move past my mistakes and character flaws to this moment?"

"Um, me?"

"You. Only you," Arthur said, kissing her cheek. "The greatest lightbulb moment of my many trips here to see Mr. V was when I was starting my third month in the experience. I was planting sunflowers out back, thinking about how tall the seeds would one day grow, and I realized that I was but a seed when we met and that you nurtured me into someone who could stand tall against all elements. *You are my fourth mentor, Akilah.*"

Now it was Akilah's turn to blush.

"Yay, Mommy!" Both Orly and Justin applauded and this time it was Mr. P, Mr. V, and Arthur who joined in.

"I don't know what to say," Akilah said.

"You don't have to say anything, dear. Just know that I love you and appreciate all the things you do and have done for me and the kids—even if there were days I didn't necessarily do a good job of communicating it or letting you know somehow."

"Wow" was all Akilah could say.

When the festivities ended and the food was put away, the grown-ups found Orly and Justin fast asleep in the mess of pillows and blankets that they had built into a fort in a corner of the living room. Rather than wake them, Clemente and Jonathan suggested letting them sleep. Jonathan said he would stay behind and sleep on the couch; he urged his young friends to go back to the motel and enjoy a parent's delight: a quiet night to themselves.

And they did.

12

Loving the Marshmallow Wife (and Kids)

Two years after his final meeting with Clemente Vivanco, Arthur had a new *aha!* moment.

During his graduation party, Arthur saw Mr. P and Mr. V quietly talking. What they discussed was none of Arthur's business . . . at least not until long after he and Akilah returned the next day to pick up the kids (and Jonathan) and say their good-byes to Clemente.

As it turned out, Jonathan had spent the last two years searching for an opportunity to slow down his own merry-go-round life of nonstop travel and new business ventures.

Mr. P wanted Arthur to take over day-to-day operations at his own company, New Beginnings, Inc.

It suddenly occurred to Arthur that everything in his life since he first met Mr. P had been leading up to this momentous opportunity.

And that's why Arthur told Jonathan . . .

"No."

"No?"

"No, thank you?"

Arthur realized that everything good in his life started with working for Jonathan Patient but grew exponentially when Akilah proposed to him. She not only loved him, but embraced marshmallow logic and its applications in ways he never even considered.

With the twins in school and Just Ask up to four locations (including St. Petersburg and Lake Buena Vista), he was just now getting to spend quality time with his wife and getting to know her as a real person—the one with whom he would grow old. He didn't for a moment seriously consider the opportunity.

"No?" Jonathan asked again, clearly surprised. If he ever considered that Arthur would turn him down, there was no evidence of that on his face.

"No," Arthur repeated for the third time.

"Shouldn't you at least take a day to think it over? Maybe talk to Akilah about it?"

"Yes," Arthur said. "And no. My answer will still be no."

And he did discuss it that very evening with Akilah when she came home from Just Ask's corporate headquarters. She was impressed by the offer, but she, too, didn't want him to accept it.

"That's why I told Jonathan 'no,'" Arthur said.

"Wait—you said 'no' without talking to me first?"

Akilah felt a wave of anger and resentment rising within her. It was an emotion she hadn't experienced toward her husband in more than two years.

"Yes—but then I realized that was a mistake, as did Jonathan. But I felt confident that we'd be of one mind on this."

"And we are," Akilah said, feeling the tension ebb away as quickly as it had come on. She hoped Arthur hadn't noticed.

The next day, Arthur reported back to Jonathan Patient that the official answer was still "no"—from them both.

But Jonathan, having recovered from his initial disappointment, made a counterproposal.

"I'd like you—and Akilah—to join my board of directors and help me pick a new CEO."

"I'll have to get back to you on that, Jonathan," Arthur said. "After I consult with my own CEO."

"I thought you might say that," Mr. P said, chuckling.

Joining the board was something Arthur and Akilah decided they *could* fit into their busy lifestyle. Moreover, they felt a responsibility to Mr. P, who had done so much for them and asked so little in return.

Arthur had a second order of business to discuss with Akilah, a new job proposal of his own: "Turn management of the restaurants over to the staff you have trained and grown to trust," he said, causing Akilah's jaw to fall to the floor.

"Why would I want to do that?"

"So you can join me as a professional speaker and help me share the marshmallow theory all around the world."

Akilah flung her arms around Arthur and squeezed tight.

"I do!"

"You mean, 'I will.'"

"No, I mean 'I do,' as in I accept your hand in business, just as I did in marriage. What took you so long to ask, silly?"

"I am learning, I am learning," he said, and they both started laughing.

Joachim's Post-Parable Analysis: Learn to Share the Marshmallow Life

We sometimes become so concentrated in one aspect of our lives that we become unbalanced in the rest, which is exactly what happened to our friend Arthur in the story you just read.

Until he met Clemente Vivanco, Arthur was guilty of paying attention to just one aspect of his life—business— and that caused him to falter as a husband and father.

It also affected his greater well-being. He allowed stress

to take hold of him. He lost control of his diet and failed to exercise in ways that might have tempered his out-of-control eating habits.

It's important to maintain a balance in all you do.

There are *five* essential elements of well-being: financial, career, physical, community, and social well-being.

Our modern world is a highly competitive, connected place. We have tremendous temptation to simply go to work and abandon the rest. For example, technology is wonderful, but we are so consumed by it that many families no longer do something as simple and satisfying as getting together for dinner each evening to discuss how their day went. Everyone these days seems to have a smartphone or an iPad to distract them and these devices intrude everywhere. Forget about what your friend from high school is up to a thousand miles away and find out what your son or daughter, seated across from you, did in school today!

Many of us have forsaken real social, personal interaction for cold, impersonal, technological intercourse.

I have seen situations where people are side-by-side in adjacent office cubicles and all they have to do to talk to each other face-to-face is stand up. But instead, they're e-mailing each other. Really? *Really?*

I have seen situations where a father hasn't had one

meaningful conversation with his son or daughter in a week, a month, or even in years. This has to stop or we are risking the very fabric of our society.

Too much of a good thing is always bad. Don't allow any good thing to take away from the balance that we all need in life.

Achieving well-being and being social requires an effort. It will not happen by accident.

Look at your week in a broad, holistic way. "Tuesday, I should call my mother or go to my daughter's home or visit with my family. Wednesday would be a good one for community service. Thursday would be a good day—just before payday—to dedicate one hour to my finances."

Balance your life on a weekly basis even though you *program* your priorities on a daily basis.

•   •   •

More than forty years have passed since the famous marshmallow experiment. Dr. Mischel—although a rather elderly gentleman as of this writing—and some of his colleagues are still following some participants of the original research project. (I duplicated the marshmallow experiment five years ago with four- and five-year-olds in Colombia; I still have several years to go before my first follow-up with those kids. Go to www.ted.com, search for my name, and you can watch my TED Talk and see video from my own marshmallow experiment.)

In an article published in the *Proceedings of the National Academy of Sciences* (PNAS), the Mischel team reported that the children's differences in self-control were still evident after forty years. There was also new information about why some people's brains may be less well developed at self-discipline and controlling their impulses.

They devised a new two-part experiment to test this. In part one, they looked for more subtle behavioral differences among the "high delayers." In other words, they compared the ones who had not eaten the marshmallow in the original experiment with the "low delayers," those who couldn't resist the temptation and ate the marshmallow. The experimenters were testing whether positive social cues would be more difficult for the kids who ate the marshmallow, the low delayers. They found fifty-nine of the 643 kids who participated in the original experiment, now with an average age of forty-six. Some of these participants were able to resist the marshmallow when they were children, and some weren't; there was a mixture of both high delayers and low delayers.

The now-adult men and women were told to press a button when they saw a face of a particular gender on a laptop computer screen as male and female faces flashed at random. In the first part of the experiment, these faces had neutral expressions. In the second part, the faces were either happy or unhappy. The accuracy with which each participant clicked on the face was then calculated.

All participants clicked accurately when the faces were neutral. However, low delayers were much less accurate when the faces showed emotion. This effect was almost entirely due to a false alarm when a happy face was shown; that is, low delayers often clicked the button when the face was happy, no matter which gender it was. High delayers, on the other hand, rarely made this mistake.

The psychologists believe that while the high delayers were able to separate emotion from gender, the happy faces were just too compelling for low delayers to resist. The neutral faces didn't cause this particular problem, indicating some aspect of impulse control is directly related to the stimuli one has to resist.

Furthermore, the subjects' behavior in this experiment was found to correlate directly to their behavior in the marshmallow experiment four decades earlier. All of which led researchers to this conclusion: Self-control is clearly stable over time unless you know how to change the wiring in your brain.

In the second part of the experiment, the subjects performed a similar test, but this time they were inside a functional magnetic resonance imaging (fMRI) machine and clinicians studied the brain activity of the high and low delayers. When the subjects suppressed the urge to press the button (when the face was of the wrong gender), an area of the brain called the right inferior frontal gyrus was active. The psychologists found that there was much less activity in the low delayers' brains than in those of the high delayers.

Instead, the ventral striatum in the low delayers became particularly active at this moment; the ventral striatum is part of the limbic system, and it deals with the way our brain processes rewards. In those with low self-control—the ones who ate the marshmallow—instead of the right inferior frontal gyrus being able to hold off temptation, the ventral striatum went crazy, entering overdrive mode, and the person had great difficulty ignoring the attraction. Low delayers, it appeared, were much more sensitive to positive social cues and had trouble suppressing them in order to deal with additional information.

In their wonderful book *Willpower*, researchers Roy F. Baumeister and John Tierney mention a 2010 study published by researchers in New Zealand that provides strong evidence of the marshmallow effect.

In a careful and long-term study, larger than anything done before, these researchers tracked one thousand children in New Zealand from the moment they were born until they turned thirty-two. Each kid's self-control was scored in a variety of ways (observation by researchers, problem reports from teachers, parents, and even the children themselves). The result was a reliable measure of children's self-discipline or self-control, and the scientists were able to check it against a wide array of outcomes all the way to adulthood. The children with high self-control grew up into adults who, in general, had better physical health, including lower rates of being overweight, fewer sexually transmitted diseases, and—lo and behold—even better dental health. (It seems that if you have self-discipline, you will floss and brush your teeth regularly.) Surprisingly, self-control was not relevant to adult depression but its lack thereof made people more prone to having problems controlling alcohol and drug use.

The children with poor self-discipline tended to end up financially challenged. They had the lower paying jobs, little or no money in the bank, and were less likely to own their own homes or have saved enough money to retire comfortably.

Interestingly, they grew up to have more children being raised by only one parent, because for them it was harder to adapt to the discipline and sacrifice required for a long-term relationship.

The children with self-discipline were much more likely to be in a stable marriage when they came from a stable two-parent home.

Sadly, the children with poor self-discipline were more likely to end up in jail. Among those with the lowest levels of self-control, more than 40 percent had a criminal conviction by age thirty-two compared with only 12 percent of the children who had not eaten the marshmallow for the longest time. In other words, they were toward the high end of self-control distribution in their younger years.

Not too surprisingly, some of these differences were correlated with intelligence, social class, and race—but these results remained significant even when those factors were considered. In a follow-up study, these same scientists were so fascinated by the findings that they decided to look at brothers and sisters from the same families to see what they would discover by studying children who had the same parents and grew up in similar homes. It was clear, over and over, that the sibling with the lower self-control during childhood did much worse during adulthood. They ended up sicker, with less money, and higher probabilities of landing in prison for some period of time.

Self-control is a necessary strength and possibly *the* key to a successful and happier life.

I do believe that more research is needed. Behavioral

scientists must be able to identify the particular brain regions that allow some people to delay gratification and control their temper or emotions. They also should conduct as many tests as needed to search for the specific hereditary characteristics that play a part in the ability to not eat the marshmallow now, but rather wait for a second marshmallow.

When I studied psychology, more years ago than I want to remember, it was believed that intelligence (IQ) was the most important variable in predicting success. Now, I strongly believe that intelligence is not as important as self-discipline, self-control, and emotional intelligence.

Some psychologists argue that what the marshmallow experiment measures most is much more than willpower or self-control. It actually tells us how the successful kids found a way to get that second marshmallow. In other words, their thinking was "I want to get that other marshmallow; what do I need to do to get it?" There were kids who knew that their willpower wasn't strong enough so instead of looking at the marshmallow or licking it (they knew if they did this, they would not be able to resist the temptation) they focused their attention on something else: playing with their pants or skirts, going under the table, looking at the walls, imagining that they were on a beach, etc. They felt they couldn't control their instincts but they knew how to control their thinking and what they could do to hold off on eating the marshmallow treat.

Luckily, the rolling, long-term study in New Zealand gives us significant new information about self-discipline and self-control and allows us to understand why some people, throughout their lives, have great difficulty resisting the temptation of the marshmallow.

● ● ●

In a 2011 study, researchers led by Larry Rosen, a psychology professor at California State University, randomly assigned 185 young college students with A and B grade averages to watch a video lecture. They knew they would be tested on its content later. During important parts of the lecture, the researchers texted each student either four or eight times with questions that had nothing to do with the lecture and asked them to respond right away. Some students were not texted at all.

Students who received eight text messages scored more than 10 percent lower on the test, which means that their grades would be one full letter lower; in other words, a C instead of a B or a B instead of an A.

The students' response times to the text messages also made a big difference in how well they performed in the test. Students who answered the texted questions within five minutes of receiving them, while important material was being discussed, provided 75 percent or fewer right answers, while those who held off five minutes or more scored over 85 percent.

Other researchers at the University of Pittsburgh, led by Flora Wei, found that students with greater self-control—in other words, those who didn't eat the marshmallow—were less likely to text in class and more likely to concentrate on the class.

This said, I don't think that in this day and age, you can eliminate technology and other distractions. They are a constant presence in the lives of students and adults alike. What we need to do is teach skills to help people understand when and how to use technology, when and how to concentrate on important stuff and not allow distractions to affect their concentration on stuff that really matters.

I don't want you to think I am knocking technology. I am not. In fact, if you don't become proficient in the use of computers, laptops, smartphones, iPads, and tablets, you will not be able to reach many of your goals. It is possible you might not even be able to reach your next appointment or event because you'll get lost without your GPS!

Never in history has technology been accessible to virtually everyone. There are now laptops that cost $100 and they are being introduced all over the Third and Fourth

World. This development will give advantages to talented people in countries where their ideas and potential would otherwise be lost forever.

All this marvelous technology is even helping business-people get money to fund their companies or projects.

Let me give you an example:

An engineer named Eric Migicovsky had a great idea. He wanted to develop a line of wristwatches that could take information from an iPhone—including text messages and caller ID for phone calls—and display it on a wristwatch he calls "Pebble."

Eric first tried the traditional route to get money: He asked family, friends, and venture capitalists to finance his company.

When that effort floundered, he turned to Kickstarter .com, a crowd-sourcing website where entrepreneurs appeal to ordinary people to back creative projects.

For pledging $99, backers were promised a Pebble watch in return.

In the first few hours after his project went live on the site, Eric had hit his original stated goal of $100,000. By nightfall, he was at $600,000 and went to a bar to celebrate with friends. By morning, the Pebble watch had drawn one million dollars. Soon he easily surpassed the former Kickstarter record of $3.3 million in funding, eventually leaping to an astounding $10 million!

There are other crowd-sourcing sites that can help people raise money, including Crowdtilt.com (general group funding), Zokos.com (for throwing a party), and Gambitious .com (for independent game developers).

I know how many people are frustrated by the enduring worldwide recession, the loss of jobs and opportunities.

You must reject this as defeatist and choose not to participate in this cloud of negativity.

There is not an *economic* crisis; there is a crisis in our lack of motivation and positive attitude! Every day people are inventing, selling, creating, and researching ideas, methods, and processes that will change lives—theirs and ours.

Let me offer a personal example:

Many years ago, I was sitting on a flight to New York from San Juan, Puerto Rico, reading a wonderful book titled *Emotional Intelligence* by Daniel Goleman. I enjoyed the book and found myself on a page that described Dr. Walter Mischel's marshmallow experiment. It spoke to me in ways little else ever had and I had a thought: Self-discipline, the ability to delay gratification, is the most important factor for success. And yet Goleman only devoted one page to it? How could that be?

At that precise moment I had one single idea: I have to write a book about this! That was how *Don't Eat the Marshmallow . . . Yet!* was born. The *Marshmallow* series has sold more than three *million* copies in twenty languages all over the world. Can you imagine how many people's lives have changed after they have learned about the principle?

How many thousands of psychologists or even millions of people had read Dr. Goleman's book? And yet, one moment's inspiration that I took away from it became the most important success of my career.

It is all about one applied idea; it is all about having self-confidence and persistence.

Jeff Bezos was a guy working on Wall Street and he had one single idea. Create the largest bookstore in the world. He quit his job and risked everything for it.

I met Jeff and his dad, Miguel, at a TED conference. They are super guys, always willing to contribute to noble causes, and are sponsors of TED, which is a magnificent venue for ideas worth sharing.

Jeff was adopted by Miguel when he was very young and it was Jeff who decided to change his name to Bezos because Miguel became Jeff's real father. When Jeff started his company, he needed funding and he went to Miguel. An engineer who had left Cuba to seek freedom in the U.S., Miguel did well as an engineer but was not a rich guy. Because of that, Jeff had second thoughts about asking his dad for the money since it was a risky venture—to say the least. But Miguel had total trust in Jeff and gave him every penny that he could.

That long shot is now worth billions upon billions in Amazon stock and Miguel is quite the proud father.

Two other interesting characters I met at TED: Larry Page and Sergey Brin.

These guys, who met at Stanford in their early twenties, started collaborating on a search engine they called "Back-Rub." It operated on Stanford servers for more than a year until they started taking up so much bandwidth that the university told them to move someplace else.

They didn't like the name too much and after brainstorming came up with Google, a play on "googol," a mathematical term for the number represented by the numeral 1 followed by 100 zeros. This number represents their one idea: Organize all the information in the world and make it accessible to everyone.

These two guys changed the world and it was all the product of one single applied idea.

I also met Microsoft cofounder Bill Gates at TED, and I will never forget when interviewer Chris Anderson, editor of *Wired* magazine, asked him how he wanted his eventual tombstone to read.

"Check my pulse," he said.

The guy was so positive that he wanted to make sure he was dead before they buried him.

In another interview, Gates was asked, "What challenge do you most fear?"

"I fear someone in a garage devising something completely new," he answered.

That was exactly what Steve Jobs and Steve Wozniak did. They started their careers in a garage, inventing a device that allowed them to make long-distance telephone calls for free. It's true: The geniuses behind Apple originally wanted nothing more than to cheat AT&T out of long-distance fees. Luckily for the world, they went on to invent and inspire a generation of products—the Macintosh computer, iPod, iPhone, and iPad—that revolutionized the world.

Steve Job's death in 2011 was a huge emotional and intellectual blow to humanity. He had so much more to contribute.

Words from one of his last speeches really resonate for me: "If you live each day as if it was your last, someday you'll most certainly be right."

In the last few years of his life, Jobs said that he looked at himself in the mirror and asked the following question:

"'If today were the last day of my life, would I want to do what I am about to do today?' And whenever the answer has been 'no' for too many days in a row, I know I need to change something."

And he then added: "Remembering that I will be dead soon is the most important tool I have encountered to help me make the big choices in life. Because almost everything— external expectations, all pride, all fear of embarrassment or failure—these things just fall away in the face of death, leaving only what is truly important."

Successful ideas sometimes arise from tragedies.

In 2001, a Texas woman named Andrea Yates drowned her five children in her bathtub. Who could imagine what psychotic thoughts went through her head when she committed such a despicable act?

A man who had been unemployed for more than a year saw news reports of Yates's atrocities and said to his mother, "Can you imagine a woman being so desperate that she would hurt her own children?"

At the time, he owed his mother more than thirty thousand dollars.

His mother astounded him with her answer: "I have been there," she said.

Once he recovered from his shock, the young man was

inspired to write a television script about what desperate women often endure.

Marc Cherry called his show *Desperate Housewives.* Maybe you've heard of it?

• • •

Psychologist Shawn Achor is a Harvard graduate and professor who wrote *The Happiness Advantage: The Seven Principles of Positive Psychology That Fuel Success and Performance at Work.* Achor suggests we take five actions every day. He assures us that doing this for twenty-one days will, in fact, rewire our brain:

1. *Write* down three gratitudes per day, three new things you are grateful for every day.

2. *Journal* about a new positive experience you have had in the past twenty-four hours.

3. *Exercise* daily.

4. *Meditate* for at least fifteen minutes a day.

5. *Commit* random acts of kindness every single day. I am good at this one; I consciously do it every single day. Whenever I see someone do something positive for someone else, I reward that person with one of my

mini-motivational books. This reinforces the behavior in people and it has a cumulative effect in our society.

* * *

I want to close with a secret.

In June 2009, Telefónica put on a special event in Tarragona, Spain, for its most important clients.

Invitations to the event included a short video describing a bottle that had been thrown into the sea with an important message inside. The bottle had a GPS transmitter, and attendees to the event could follow the bottle's progress online as it floated toward Tarragona.

This creative idea increased participants' interest and everyone wanted to attend the event to see if the bottle would arrive on time.

After twenty days at sea, after traveling more than 150 miles, the bottle arrived in Tarragona right in the middle of the convention.

An enormous video screen showed a view of the beach with someone waiting for the bottle. It arrived and the gentleman who retrieved it handed it off to another person, who took the bottle into the main ballroom where everyone's attention was riveted on learning of its historic contents.

There was total silence as the bottle was given to the

master of ceremonies. She opened it to great anticipation and read its very important message[3]:

> Let's not pretend that things will change if we keep doing the same things. A crisis can be a real blessing to any person, to any nation. For all crises bring progress.
>
> Creativity is born from anguish. Just like the day is born from the dark night. It's in crisis that invention is born, as well as discoveries, and big strategies. Who overcomes crisis, overcomes himself, without getting overcome. Who blames his failure to a crisis neglects his own talent, and is more respectful to problems than to solutions. Incompetence is the true crisis.
>
> The greatest inconvenience of people and nations is the laziness with which they attempt to find the solutions to their problems. There's no challenge without a crisis. Without challenges, life becomes a routine, a slow agony. There's no merit without crisis. It's in the crisis where we can show the very best in us. Without a crisis, any wind becomes a tender touch. To speak about a crisis is to promote it. Not to speak about it is to exalt conformism. Let us work hard instead.

[3] The English translation of Einstein's words come from *Nanotechnology: balancing the promises* by Víctor Puntes and Josep Saldaña (Catalan Institute of Nanotechnology, 2009) http://www.lulu.com/shop/v%C3%ADctor-puntes-and -josep-salda%C3%B1a/nanotechnology-balancing-the-promises/paperback/ product-17800198.html;jsessionid=9E12708773CB59B94BB9D9CDBA5043AD.

Let us stop, once and for all, the menacing crisis that represents the tragedy of not being willing to overcome it.

After hearing those words—originally spoken by famed mathematician and scientist Albert Einstein—no one at that business conference spoke about any existing crisis, they just spoke about opportunity. It was a truly inspiring moment of humanity, technology, and the world in which we live, breathe—and sometimes tread water.

You and I must look at life the way the brilliant Einstein did, as a constant challenge, full of unbridled opportunity, and we must all practice the marshmallow principles and stories we have shared in these pages.

If you do that, you will always come out ahead, that is for sure.

Good luck to us all!